Fat-Quarter QUILTING

21 Terrific 16" x 20" Projects

Lori Smith

Martingale®
& COMPANY

Fat-Quarter Quilting:
21 Terrific 16" x 20" Projects
© 2009 by Lori Smith

That Patchwork Place® is an imprint of
Martingale & Company®.

Martingale & Company
20205 144th Ave. NE
Woodinville, WA 98072-8478 USA
www.martingale-pub.com

Credits

President & CEO: Tom Wierzbicki

Editor in Chief: Mary V. Green

Managing Editor: Tina Cook

Technical Editor: Ellen Pahl

Copy Editor: Marcy Heffernan

Design Director: Stan Green

Production Manager: Regina Girard

Illustrator: Adrienne Smitke

Cover & Text Designer: Stan Green

Photographer: Brent Kane

Printed in China
14 13 12 11 10 09   8 7 6 5 4 3 2

Library of Congress Cataloging-in-Publication Data
Library of Congress Control Number: 2009017856

ISBN: 978-1-56477-946-5

Mission Statement

Dedicated to providing quality products and service to inspire creativity.

Dedication

This book is dedicated to all of the quilters who continue
to support my work. Thank you.

Lori

Contents

PAGE 18

PAGE 22

PAGE 60

PAGE 85

Introduction

Who can resist the temptation of adding just one more fat quarter to their stash?

Fat-Quarter Quilting is a collection of fun, fast, and easy quilt patterns perfect for that abundant fat-quarter collection waiting to be used. Creating these small treasures can be almost as addictive as collecting the fabric! Correlating with the measurement of fat quarters, all quilts finish 16" x 20" when complete.

Creating small quilts provides a wonderful opportunity to experience the ease and exhilaration of creating a quilt without the constraints and inhibitions of working within a much larger format. Our quilting ancestors have provided an endless resource of traditional quilt-block patterns that we have often longed to make yet have not found the time to explore. Small quilts

provide the perfect opportunity to create those historical treasures.

There are so many fabrics to choose from yet so little time to use them all. Small quilts provide a wonderful opportunity to play and experiment with fabrics, prints, and color combinations we may have never considered using in a larger quilt. What better way to develop your color confidence than to create these small wonders?

It's time to explore the freedom, ease of creating, and endless design possibilities that small quilts offer in pattern, color, fabric selection, technique, and setting arrangement. Enjoy making one or all!

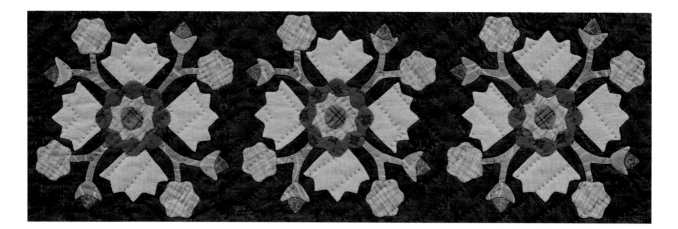

Nine Patch Nostalgia

The traditional Nine Patch block honors our quilting heritage; it is simple yet many beautiful designs can be created with it. Setting the blocks on point provides a wonderful opportunity to highlight a collection of homespuns reminiscent of yesteryear. Of course, it would be perfect for using other reproduction fabrics as well.

Finished quilt: 16" x 20"
Finished block: 3" x 3"

Materials

1 fat quarter of red print for blocks
1 fat quarter of medium green fabric for
    setting triangles
1 fat eighth of medium plaid for alternate
    blocks
1 fat eighth of dark plaid for border
1 fat eighth of off-white print for blocks
1 fat eighth of light green fabric for
    alternate blocks
1 fat quarter of fabric for binding
1 fat quarter of fabric for backing
18" x 22" piece of batting

Cutting

From the red print, cut:
60 squares, 1½" x 1½"

From the off-white print, cut:
48 squares, 1½" x 1½"

From the light green fabric, cut:
3 squares, 3⅞" x 3⅞"; cut once diagonally to make
    6 triangles
1 square, 4¼" x 4¼"; cut twice diagonally to make
    4 triangles

From the medium green fabric, cut:
2 squares, 3" x 3"; cut once diagonally to make
    4 triangles
3 squares, 5½" x 5½"; cut twice diagonally to make
    12 triangles (2 are extra)

From the medium plaid, cut:
2 squares, 3" x 3"; cut once diagonally to make 4
    triangles
1 square, 5½" x 5½"; cut twice diagonally to make
    4 triangles (2 are extra)

From the dark plaid, cut:
2 strips, 2⅛" x 20½"
2 strips, 2" x 13¼"

From the binding fabric, cut:
4 strips, 1¾" x 20"

Making the Blocks

1. Sew four off-white squares and five red squares together as shown to make a Nine Patch block. Make 12 blocks.

Make 12.

2. Sew a light green 4¼" triangle to a plaid 3" triangle along the short edges; press. Sew this unit to the light green 3⅞" triangle. Make two blocks. Repeat to make two more blocks, changing the orientation of the smaller triangles

 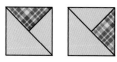

Make 2 of each.

3. Sew a light green 3⅞" triangle to a plaid 5½" triangle to make a half-square-triangle unit. Press the seam allowances toward the plaid triangle. Make two half-square-triangle units.

Make 2.

Assembling the Quilt

1. Arrange the Nine Patch blocks, the medium green triangles, the blocks from step 2, and the units from step 3 in diagonal rows as shown in the assembly diagram.

2. Sew the blocks and units into rows, pressing seam allowances toward the triangles and alternate blocks. Sew the rows together and press the seam allowances in one direction.

3. Sew the plaid 2" x 13¼" border strips to the top and bottom of the quilt. Press toward the border strips. Add the plaid 2⅛" x 20½" border strips to the sides of the quilt.

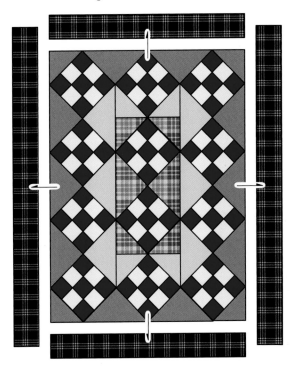

4. Layer the quilt with backing and batting. Baste the layers together and quilt as desired. Add the binding and enjoy.

Friends Remembered

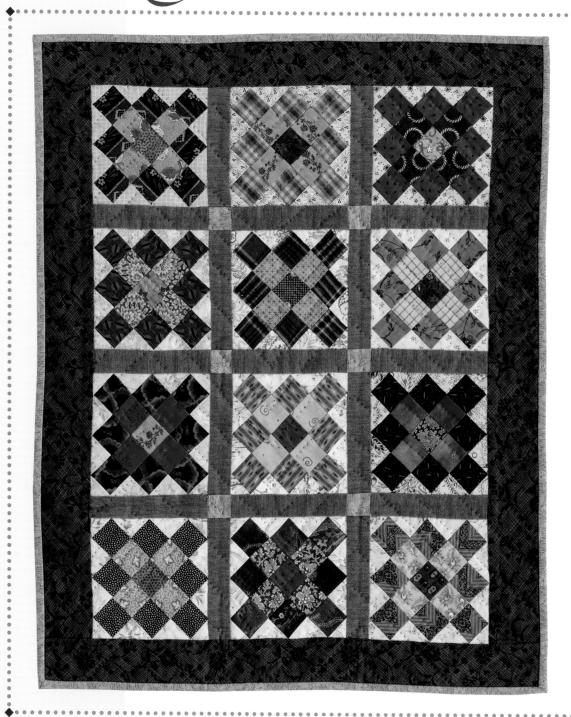

Sharing the love of quilting is a time-honored tradition. Friendship quilts were traditionally signature quilts made to be given to friends or loved ones and were popular during America's westward expansion. Swap charm squares with others or utilize remnants from previous quilts to create your own memorable quilt.

Finished quilt: 16" x 20"
Finished block: 3¾" x 3¾"

Materials

1 fat eighth of dark brown print for border
1 fat eighth of medium brown print for
    sashing
3 fat eighths *total* of assorted dark,
    medium, and light-medium prints for
    blocks
1 fat quarter *total* of assorted light
    background prints for blocks
1 fat quarter of rose print for sashing
    squares and binding
1 fat quarter of fabric for backing
18" x 22" piece of batting

Cutting

*Each block is made from 3 different print fabrics
and a background fabric. Cut the pieces as indicated for each block. Repeat the cutting directions to
make 12 blocks, keeping the fabrics for each
block separate. For a paper-piecing option, cut the
pieces oversized as noted and refer to "Paper
Piecing the Album Block" on page 12.*

FOR ONE BLOCK
From a dark to medium print, cut:
8 squares, 1⅜" x 1⅜"★

From a medium or light-medium print, cut:
4 squares, 1⅜" x 1⅜"★

**From a contrasting dark or medium print,
cut:**
1 square, 1⅜" x 1⅜"★

From a light background print, cut:
2 squares, 1½" x 1½"; cut once diagonally to make
    4 triangles★
2 squares, 2½" x 2½"; cut twice diagonally to
    make 8 triangles★★

**FOR SASHING, BORDERS,
AND BINDING**
From a medium brown print, cut:
17 rectangles, 1¼" x 4¼"

From the rose print, cut:
6 squares, 1¼" x 1¼"

From the dark brown print, cut:
2 strips, 1⅞" x 16½"
2 strips, 2⅛" x 17¾"

From the binding fabric, cut:
4 strips, 1¾" x 20"

★Cut these squares 2" x 2" for paper piecing.
★★Cut these squares 3" x 3" for paper piecing.

Making the Blocks

1. Arrange the squares and triangles for one block
in diagonal rows as shown. Sew the squares and
triangles in rows, pressing seam allowances as
indicated by the arrows in the diagram.

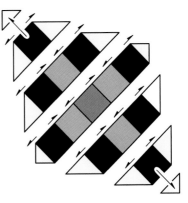

2. Use a shorter-than-normal stitch length to sew the rows together. Press the seam allowances open to reduce bulk. The block should measure 4¼" x 4¼".

3. Repeat steps 1 and 2 to make a total of 12 blocks.

Assembling the Quilt

1. Arrange the blocks, medium brown sashing rectangles, and rose sashing squares on a design wall, referring to the quilt assembly diagram.

2. Sew the blocks, sashing, and sashing squares into rows as shown. Press all seam allowances toward the sashing.

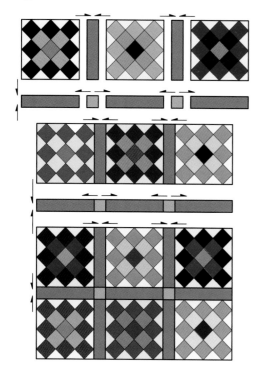

3. Sew the rows together. Press the seam allowances toward the sashing rows.

4. Sew the dark brown 2⅛" x 17¾" border strips to the sides of the quilt. Press seam allowances toward the borders. Sew the dark brown 1⅞" x 16½" border strips to the top and bottom; press.

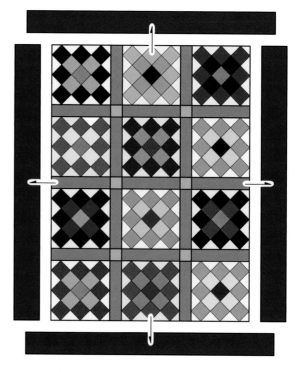

5. Layer the quilt top, batting, and backing. Baste the layers together and quilt as desired. Add the binding and enjoy.

Paper Piecing the Album Block

If you prefer, you can paper piece the Album block using the pattern on page 13. For ease when paper-foundation piecing, cut the patches for the block oversized as noted below the cutting list on page 11.

1. Make 12 copies of the patterns on page 13. The numbers on each pattern piece indicate the sewing order.

2. Piece the block in diagonal rows, beginning with piece 1 in each row. Trim and press the seam allowances after sewing each seam.

3. Sew the rows together. Trim the block and remove the paper foundation.

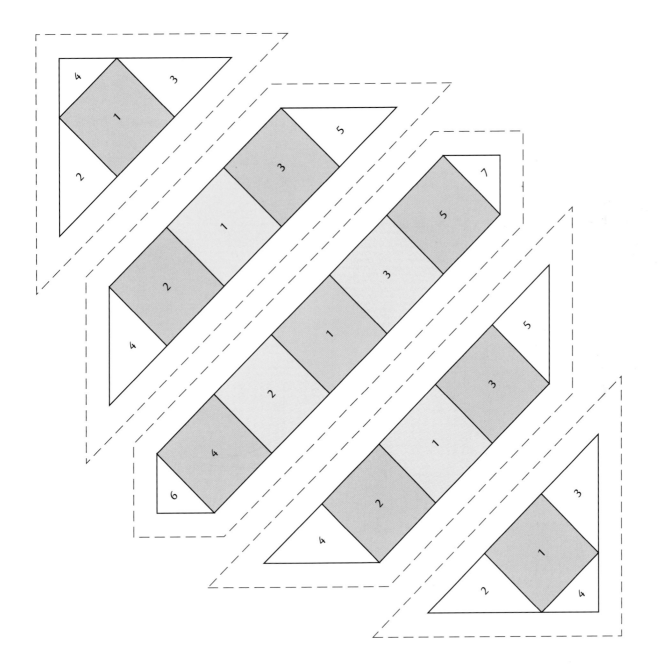

Medallion Star

Medallion quilts have a long history in quilting tradition, being one of the earliest quilting styles. The shapes within the central block are repeated throughout the borders, unifying the overall design of the quilt. Created from a collection of reproduction fabrics, this quilt is sure to become a family keepsake.

Finished quilt: 16" x 20"
Finished block: 6" x 6"

Materials

3 fat quarters *total* of assorted medium
    to dark prints in blues, greens, reds,
    pinks, and browns for block and
    borders
2 fat quarters *total* of assorted light to
    medium-light prints for block and
    borders
1 fat quarter of fabric for binding
1 fat quarter of fabric for backing
18" x 22" piece of batting

Cutting

Center Star Block

From *1* red print, cut:
2 squares, 2⅞" x 2⅞"; cut once diagonally to
    make 4 triangles

From *1* light print, cut:
1 square, 3¼" x 3¼"; cut twice diagonally to make
    4 triangles
2 squares, 2⅞"x 2⅞"; cut once diagonally to make
    4 triangles

From *1* dark green print, cut:
1 square, 3¼" x 3¼"; cut twice diagonally to make
    4 triangles

From *1* medium green print, cut:
2 squares, 3¼" x 3¼"; cut twice diagonally to
    make 8 triangles

From *1* blue print, cut:
1 square, 2½" x 2½"

Pieced Rows and Binding

**From the assorted light to medium-light
prints, cut:**
16 squares, 1½" x 1½"
22 squares, 1⅞" x 1⅞"; cut once diagonally to
    make 44 triangles

**From the assorted medium to dark prints,
cut:**
16 squares, 1½" x 1½"
22 squares, 1⅞" x 1⅞"; cut once diagonally to
    make 44 triangles
8 squares, 2½" x 2½"
16 squares, 2⅞" x 2⅞"; cut once diagonally to
    make 32 triangles

**From the assorted light, medium, and dark
prints, cut:**
12 squares, 3¼" x 3¼"; cut twice diagonally to
    make 48 triangles

**From the assorted light to medium-light
prints, cut:**
16 squares, 2⅞" x 2⅞"; cut once diagonally to
    make 32 triangles

From the binding fabric, cut:
4 strips, 1¾" x 20"

Making the Center Star Block

1. Sew a red 2⅞" triangle to a light 2⅞" triangle to
make a half-square-triangle unit. Press toward the
red print. Make four half-square-triangle units.

Make 4.

2. Sew the dark green, medium green, and light
3¼" triangles together as shown. Make four units.

Make 4.

3. Sew the units from steps 1 and 2 and the blue
2½" square together in rows as shown. Sew the
rows together to make the Center Star block.

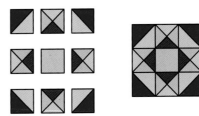

Making the Four-Patch Rows

1. Sew two light 1½" squares and two medium or dark 1½" squares together as shown to make a four-patch unit. Make eight four-patch units.

Make 8.

2. Sew a dark 2½" square to opposite sides of a four-patch unit from step 1. Make two rows.

Make 2.

3. Sew three units from step 1 to two dark 2½" squares, positioning the four-patch units as shown. Make two rows.

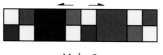

Make 2.

Making the Small Half-Square-Triangle Rows

1. Sew the medium and dark 1⅞" triangles to the light 1⅞" triangles to make 44 half-square-triangle units. Press seam allowances toward the dark triangles.

2. Sew 10 units from step 1 together as shown to make a row. Make two rows, one each for the side borders. Sew 12 units together to make a row, changing the orientation of the triangles and rotating one unit on the end as shown. Make two rows, one each for the top and bottom borders.

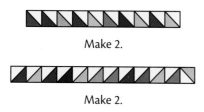

Make 2.

Make 2.

Making the Quarter-Square-Triangle Rows

1. Sew four of the assorted light, medium, and dark 3¼" triangles together to make a quarter-square-triangle unit. Make 12.

Make 12.

2. Sew six of the units from step 1 together to make a row. Make two rows.

Make 2.

Making the Large Half-Square-Triangle Rows

1. Sew together the 32 medium to dark and 32 light to medium 2⅞" triangles to make 32 half-square-triangle units. Press the seam allowances toward the darker triangles.

2. Sew eight of the units from step 1 together as shown to make a row. Make two rows, one for each of the side borders. Make another two rows, but change the orientation of the triangles and rotate the half-square-triangle unit on the end as shown.

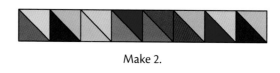

Make 2.

Make 2.

Assembling and Finishing the Quilt

1. Arrange the Center Star block and rows as shown in the assembly diagram. Sew the rows to the quilt, adding sides first, and then the top and bottom for each border row. Press the seam allowances outward after sewing each seam.

2. Layer the quilt top, batting, and backing. Baste the layers together and quilt as desired. Add the binding and enjoy.

Delectable Mountains

Enjoy a sense of the beauty of nature while climbing the mountains with this traditionally inspired quilt. A limited palette of colors and fabrics creates a soothing journey.

Finished quilt: 16" x 20"

Materials

1 fat quarter of light green floral
1 fat quarter of dark green print
1 fat quarter of violet print
1 fat quarter of off-white print
1 fat quarter of fabric for backing
18" x 22" piece of batting

Cutting

As you cut, keep all of the triangles separate and label them according to the size of the original square so that you can easily tell them apart after cutting.

From the light green floral, cut:
1 square, 2½" x 2½"
4 squares, 4⅞" x 4⅞"; cut once diagonally to make 8 triangles
1 square, 5¼" x 5¼"; cut twice diagonally to make 4 triangles

From the dark green print, cut:
4 squares, 1⅞" x 1⅞"; cut once diagonally to make 8 triangles
13 squares, 3¼" x 3¼"; cut twice diagonally to make 52 triangles
8 squares, 2⅞" x 2⅞"; cut once diagonally to make 16 triangles

From the violet print, cut:
3 squares, 5¼" x 5¼"; cut twice diagonally to make 12 triangles
8 squares, 1⅞" x 1⅞"; cut once diagonally to make 16 triangles
4 binding strips, 1¾" x 20"

From the off-white print, cut:
13 squares, 3¼" x 3¼"; cut twice diagonally to make 52 triangles
4 squares, 1½" x 1½"
4 squares, 2⅞" x 2⅞"; cut once diagonally to make 8 triangles
20 squares, 1⅞" x 1⅞"; cut once diagonally to make 40 triangles

Assembling the Quilt

1. Sew two dark green 1⅞" triangles to an off-white 3¼" triangle as shown to make a star-point unit; press. Make four star-point units.

Make 4.

2. Arrange off-white 1½" squares, the star-point units, and the light green floral 2½" square as shown. Sew the units into rows; press. Sew the rows together to make the Sawtooth Star block; press.

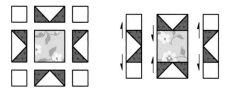

Press with Care

Many of the pieced units will have bias edges as you are constructing the quilt. Take care when sewing and pressing triangles. In the finished quilt, all of the pieces will have the straight of grain parallel with the edges of the quilt.

3. Sew a large violet triangle to each side of the Sawtooth Star block; press.

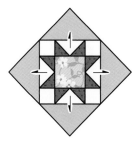

4. Sew dark green 3¼" triangles, off-white 3¼" triangles, and off-white 2⅞" triangles together in rows as shown. Make two of each row.

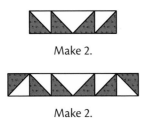

Make 2.

Make 2.

5. Sew the shorter rows from step 4 to opposite sides of the unit from step 3; press. Sew the longer rows from step 4 to the remaining sides; press.

6. Sew a large violet triangle to each side of the light green floral 4⅞" triangle; press. Make four units.

Make 4.

7. Sew dark green 3¼" triangles, off-white 3¼" triangles, and off-white 2⅞" triangles together in rows as shown. Make four of each.

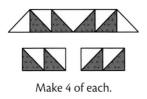

Make 4 of each.

8. Sew one of each short row from step 7 to opposite sides of the units from step 6; press. Add a long row from step 7 to one remaining side as shown; press. Make 4 units.

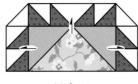

Make 4.

9. Sew a light green floral 4⅞" triangle and two light green floral 5¼" triangles to two units from step 8 as shown. Press seam allowances toward the light green floral triangles. Sew a light green floral 4⅞" triangle to the remaining two units from step 8.

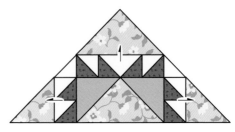

Make 2.

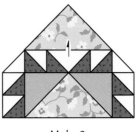

Make 2.

10. Sew one violet 1⅞" triangle and three off-white 1⅞" triangles together as shown. Add a dark green 2⅞" triangle and press. Make 12 units.

Make 12.

11. Sew two violet 1⅞" triangles, two off-white 1⅞" triangles, and two off-white 3¼" triangles together as shown; press. Sew a dark green 2⅞" triangle to each side; press.

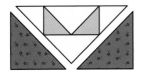

Make 2.

12. Sew the units from steps 10 and 11 together as shown. Make two rows.

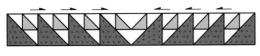

Make 2.

13. Arrange and sew the units from step 9 and the center unit in diagonal rows; press. Sew the rows together.

14. Add the units from step 12 to the top and bottom of the quilt.

15. Layer the quilt top, batting, and backing. Baste the layers together and quilt as desired. Add the binding and enjoy.

$\mathcal{B}atik$ Fun

Diamonds dance across the surface of the quilt with the careful placement of light, medium, and dark values. The use of warm and cool colors further adds to the excitement. Use some of your fabulous batiks to explore the endless design possibilities triangles and squares have to offer.

◆

> **Finished quilt: 16" x 20"**
> **Finished block: 2" x 2"**

Materials

1 fat quarter *total* of assorted light to
  medium-light batiks for blocks
1 fat quarter *total* of assorted medium
  batiks for blocks and borders
1 fat quarter *total* of assorted medium-dark
  to dark batiks for blocks and borders
1 fat quarter of fabric for binding
1 fat quarter of fabric for backing
18" x 22" piece of batting

Cutting

From the assorted light to medium-light batiks, cut:
48 squares, 1⅞" x 1⅞"; cut once diagonally to
  make 96 triangles

From the assorted medium batiks, cut:
48 squares, 1½" x 1½"
16 squares, 2⅞" x 2⅞"; cut once diagonally to
  make 32 triangles

From the assorted medium-dark to dark batiks, cut:
40 squares, 2⅞" x 2⅞"; cut once diagonally to
  make 80 triangles

From the binding fabric, cut:
4 strips, 1¾" x 20"

Making the Blocks

1. Sew a light or medium-light 1⅞" triangle to two
sides of a medium batik 1½" square as shown; press.

2. Sew the unit from step 1 to a medium-dark or
dark batik 2⅞" triangle; press. The block should
measure 2½" x 2½". Make 48 Flying Goose blocks.

Make 48.

3. Sew a medium batik 2⅞" triangle to a medium-
dark to dark batik 2⅞" triangle; press. Make 32
half-square-triangle units for the borders.

Make 32.

4. Arrange the blocks from step 2 in eight rows of
six blocks each. Sew them together in groups of
four to make a section. Sew three sections together
to make a horizontal row. Make four horizontal

Hand-Quilting Tip

Batiks can be a challenge when hand quilting, due to the close weave of the fabric. I used a mottled fabric for the backing. This provides the look of a batik, while making it easier to hand quilt.

rows and sew the rows together to make the center of the quilt. Press the seam allowances open.

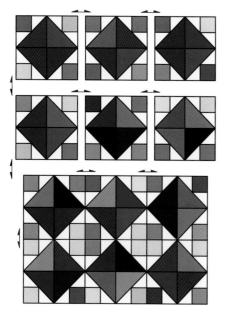

5. Arrange the half-square-triangle units around the center of the quilt, placing the base of the darker triangles along the outer edges. They will create the appearance of a sawtooth border around the quilt. Sew eight units together for each of the four borders. Press the seam allowances open.

6. Sew the borders to the sides of the quilt, and then the top and bottom. Press the seam allowances open.

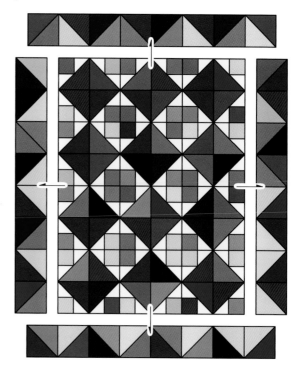

7. Layer the quilt top, batting, and backing. Baste the layers together and quilt as desired. Add the binding and enjoy.

Reproduction Row

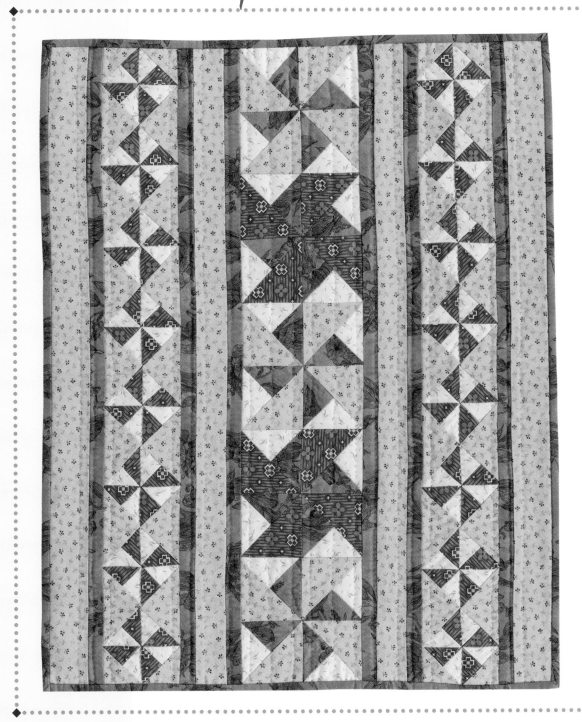

Our quilting ancestors introduced setting blocks in rows. Incorporating the Windmill and Pinwheel blocks in the design adds energy and movement while the vertical sashing stabilizes the quilt with bold, strong lines. The color scheme further enhances the appearance of a quilt that could have been made many years ago.

Finished quilt: 16" x 20"
Finished Pinwheel block: 1¾" x 1¾"
Finished Windmill block: 4" x 4"

Materials

1 fat quarter of gold print for blocks and
   sashing
1 fat eighth of red print for blocks
1 fat quarter of green print for blocks,
   sashing, and binding
1 fat quarter of light tan print for blocks
1 fat quarter of fabric for backing
18" x 22" piece of batting

Cutting

From the light tan print, cut:
32 squares, 1¾" x 1¾"; cut once diagonally
   to make 64 triangles
5 squares, 3¼" x 3¼"; cut twice diagonally
   to make 20 triangles

From the red print, cut:
32 squares, 1¾" x 1¾"; cut once diagonally
   to make 64 triangles
4 squares, 2⅞" x 2⅞"; cut once diagonally
   to make 8 triangles

From the gold print, cut:
4 strips, 1½" x 20½"
6 squares, 2⅞" x 2⅞"; cut once diagonally
   to make 12 triangles
7 squares, 3¾" x 3¾"; cut twice diagonally
   to make 28 triangles
4 squares, 2⅛" x 2⅛"; cut once diagonally
   to make 8 triangles

From the green print, cut:
5 squares, 3¼" x 3¼"; cut twice diagonally
   to make 20 triangles
6 strips, 1" x 20½"

From the binding fabric, cut:
4 strips, 1¾" x 20"

Making the Windmill Blocks

1. Sew a tan 3¼" triangle and a green 3¼" triangle together along the short sides. Make 20 units.

Make 20.

2. Sew 12 of the units from step 1 to gold 2⅞" triangles. Sew four of these units together to make the Windmill block. Repeat to make three blocks. The blocks should measure 4½" x 4½".

Make 3.

3. Sew 8 of the units from step 1 to red 2⅞" triangles. Sew these units together as you did in step 2 to make two Windmill blocks.

Make 2.

Making the Pinwheel Blocks

1. Sew a red 1¾" triangle to a tan 1¾" triangle to make a half-square-triangle unit; press. Make 64 half-square-triangle units.

2. Sew the half-square-triangle units together as shown to make 16 Pinwheel blocks.

Make 16.

Assembling and Finishing the Quilt

1. Sew eight Pinwheel blocks and 14 gold 3¾"
triangles together as shown to make a row. Add the
2⅛" triangles to the ends. Make two rows.

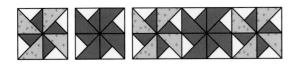

Make 2.

2. Sew the five Windmill blocks together in a row,
alternating the gold and red blocks.

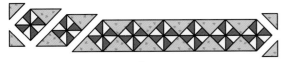

3. Sew a green 1" x 20½" strip to one side of each
gold 1½" x 20½" strip. Sew a second green strip
to the opposite side of two of the gold strips. Press
seam allowances toward the green strips.

Make 2 of each.

4. Sew the vertical rows together. Press the seam
allowances toward the green strips.

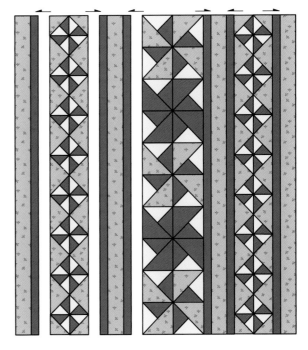

5. Layer the quilt top, batting, and backing. Baste
the layers together and quilt as desired. Add the
binding and enjoy.

Patriotism abounds with a sampling of pieced Star blocks in red, white, and blue. Create a classic row quilt that is sure to warm the hearts of those who have protected the freedoms we enjoy.

Finished quilt: 16" x 20"
Finished Star block: 4" x 4"
Finished Odd Fellow's Chain block: 8" x 8"

Materials

1 fat quarter *total* of assorted light prints for
   blocks
1 fat quarter *total* of assorted blue prints for
   blocks and outer border
2 fat quarters *total* of assorted red prints for
   blocks and borders
1 fat eighth *total* of assorted tan prints for blocks
1 fat eighth of light brown plaid for
   checkerboard border
1 fat quarter of fabric for binding
1 fat quarter of fabric for backing
18" x 22" piece of batting

Cutting

*Each block is made from different prints. Cut the
pieces as indicated for each block. Repeat the cutting
to make two of each block, keeping the fabrics for each
block separate.*

ONE ODD FELLOW'S CHAIN BLOCK

From the assorted light prints, cut:
8 squares, 1⅞" x 1⅞"; cut once diagonally to make
   16 triangles
3 squares, 3¼" x 3¼"; cut twice diagonally to
   make 12 triangles
12 squares, 1½" x 1½"

From the assorted red prints, cut:
12 squares, 1⅞" x 1⅞"; cut once diagonally to
   make 24 triangles
1 square, 2½" x 2½"

From the assorted blue prints, cut:
4 squares, 2⅞" x 2⅞"; cut once diagonally to
   make 8 triangles

ONE STAR BLOCK

From a tan print, cut:
2 squares, 1⅞" x 1⅞"; cut once diagonally to make
   4 triangles

From a red print, cut:
2 squares, 1⅞" x 1⅞"; cut once diagonally to make
   4 triangles★

From a light print, cut:
1 square, 3¼" x 3¼"; cut twice diagonally to make
   4 triangles
4 squares, 1½" x 1½"

From a blue print, cut:
4 squares, 1⅞" x 1⅞"; cut once diagonally to make
   8 triangles★

BORDERS AND BINDING

From the assorted red prints, cut:
1½"-wide strips to total 70"
10 squares, 2⅞" x 2⅞"; cut once diagonally to
   make 20 triangles

From the light brown plaid, cut:
4 strips, 1½" x 20"

From the assorted blue prints, cut:
10 squares, 2⅞" x 2⅞"; cut once diagonally to
   make 20 triangles

From the binding fabric, cut:
4 strips, 1¾" x 20"

*★For the second Star block, cut 4 squares of red and 2
squares of blue to reverse the position of the colors in
the block.*

Making the Odd Fellow's Chain Block

1. Sew a red 1⅞" triangle to each short side of a light 3¼" triangle to make a flying-geese unit; press. Repeat to make eight flying-geese units.

Make 8.

2. Arrange four of the flying-geese units from step 1 with the red 2½" square and four light 1½" squares as shown. Sew them together in rows, and sew the rows together to make the star unit.

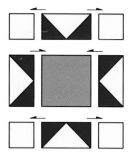

3. Sew a light 1⅞" triangle to each short side of the remaining four flying-geese units from step 1; press. Sew a light 3¼" triangle to the bottom; press. Repeat to make four units.

Make 4.

4. Sew a blue print 2⅞" triangle to each short side of the unit from step 3; press. Make four units.

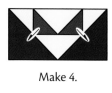

Make 4.

5. Sew a light 1⅞" triangle to a red 1⅞" triangle to make a half-square-triangle unit; press. Make eight half-square-triangle units.

6. Sew two of the half-square-triangle units from step 5 to two light 1½" squares as shown; press. Make four units.

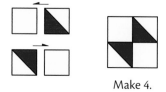

Make 4.

7. Arrange the units from steps 4 and 6 with the star unit from step 2 as shown; sew them together in rows. Sew the rows together to make the Odd Fellow's Chain block. It should measure 8½" x 8½". Press seam allowances to one side, or open to reduce bulk.

8. Repeat steps 1–7 to make the second Odd Fellow's Chain block.

Making the Star Block

1. Sew a red 1⅞" triangle to a tan 1⅞" triangle to make a half-square-triangle unit; press. Make four. Sew the four units together to make the center of the Star block.

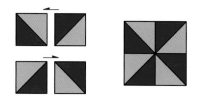

2. Sew a blue 1⅞" triangle to each short side of a light 3¼" triangle to make a flying-geese unit as shown; press. Make four flying-geese units.

Make 4.

3. Arrange the units from steps 1 and 2 with the light 1½" squares as shown. Sew them into rows, and sew the rows together to make the Star block. The block should measure 4½" x 4½".

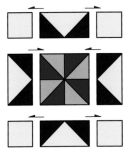

4. Repeat steps 1–3 to make a second block using the blue triangles in the center and red triangles for the star points.

Making the Borders

1. Sew the red 1½"-wide strips together to make one strip, at least 70" long. Repeat with the light brown plaid 1½" x 20" strips.
2. Sew the red and light brown plaid strips together to make a strip set. Press the seam allowances toward the red print. Cut 40 segments, 1½" wide.

1½"

Cut 40 segments.

3. Sew 20 segments from step 2 together to make the checkerboard border. Repeat to make two borders.

Make 2.

4. Sew a blue triangle to each of the red triangles to make half-square-triangle units. Make 20. Sew 10 of the units together for each border. Position the blue triangles in opposite directions for each side border as shown.

Make 1 of each.

Assembling and Finishing the Quilt

1. Sew the four blocks together as shown in the quilt assembly diagram.
2. Add a checkerboard border strip to each side; press.
3. Add the triangle borders, placing the base of the blue triangles next to the checkerboard border as shown; press.

4. Layer the quilt top, batting, and backing. Baste the layers together and quilt as desired. Add the binding and enjoy.

10-*Block* Sampler

This quilt provides a marvelous opportunity to explore and create 10 traditional quilt block patterns set in vertical rows reminiscent of quilts of yesteryear. To further enhance the aged appearance of the quilt, sew the blocks in a variety of brown, red, and cream prints with randomly cut pieces for the outer border.

> **Finished quilt: 16" x 20"**
> **Finished blocks: 4" x 4"**

Materials

1 fat quarter *total* of assorted light prints for
    blocks
1 fat quarter *total* of assorted red prints for
    blocks
1 fat quarter *total* of assorted medium and dark
    green prints for blocks
1 fat quarter *total* of assorted brown prints for
    pieced border
1 fat quarter of dark brown print for sashing
    and binding
1 fat eighth of brown floral for the center row
4" x 6" scrap of light plaid for blocks
1 fat quarter of fabric for backing
18" x 22" piece of batting

Cutting

*When cutting fabrics, I arrange the pieces for each
block on a sheet of paper as I cut. After cutting, I
move the sheets of paper, with the pieces in place, to
the sewing table.*

BASKET BLOCK

From a light print, cut:
3 squares, 1⅞" x 1⅞"; cut once diagonally to make
    6 triangles (1 is extra)
2 rectangles, 1½" x 2½"
1 square, 2⅞" x 2⅞"; cut once diagonally to make
    2 triangles (1 is extra)

From the assorted red prints, cut:
3 squares, 1⅞" x 1⅞"; cut once diagonally to make
    6 triangles (1 is extra)

From a medium green print, cut:
1 square, 2⅞" x 2⅞"; cut once diagonally to make
    2 triangles (1 is extra)

From dark green prints, cut:
1 square, 2⅞" x 2⅞"; cut once diagonally to make
    2 triangles (1 is extra)
1 square, 1⅞" x 1⅞"; cut once diagonally to make
    2 triangles

VARIABLE STAR BLOCK

From a light print, cut:
1 square, 3¼" x 3¼"; cut twice diagonally to make
    4 triangles
4 squares, 1½" x 1½"

From a green print, cut:
4 squares, 1⅞" x 1⅞"; cut once diagonally to make
    8 triangles

From a red print, cut:
1 square, 2½" x 2½"

FLOCK OF GEESE BLOCK

From a light print, cut:
4 squares, 1⅞" x 1⅞"; cut once diagonally to make
    8 triangles

From the light plaid, cut:
1 square, 2⅞" x 2⅞"; cut once diagonally to make
    2 triangles

From the red prints, cut:
4 squares, 1⅞" x 1⅞"; cut once diagonally to make
    8 triangles

From a dark green print, cut:
1 square, 2⅞" x 2⅞"; cut once diagonally to make
    2 triangles

DOUBLE X BLOCK

From a light print, cut:
5 squares, 1⅞" x 1⅞"; cut once diagonally to make
    10 triangles
2 squares, 1½" x 1½"

From the green prints, cut:
5 squares, 1⅞" x 1⅞"; cut once diagonally to make
    10 triangles

From a red print, cut:
1 square, 2½" x 2½"

BUCKEYE BEAUTY BLOCK

From a light print, cut:
1 square, 2⅞" x 2⅞"; cut once diagonally to make
  2 triangles
4 squares, 1½" x 1½"

From a green print, cut:
1 square, 2⅞" x 2⅞"; cut once diagonally to make
  2 triangles

From the red prints, cut:
4 squares, 1½" x 1½"

ANVIL BLOCK

From the light prints, cut:
2 squares, 1⅞" x 1⅞"; cut once diagonally to make
  4 triangles
2 squares, 1½" x 1½"
1 square, 2⅞" x 2⅞"; cut once diagonally to make
  2 triangles

From a medium green print, cut:
2 squares, 1½" x 1½"

From a dark green print, cut:
2 squares, 1⅞" x 1⅞"; cut once diagonally to make
  4 triangles

From a red print, cut:
1 square, 2⅞" x 2⅞"; cut once diagonally to make
  2 triangles

CHURN DASH BLOCK

From a light print, cut:
2 squares, 2⅜" x 2⅜"; cut once diagonally to
  make 4 triangles
4 rectangles, 1¼" x 1½"

From a red print, cut:
2 squares, 2⅜" x 2⅜"; cut once diagonally to
  make 4 triangles

From a dark green print, cut:
4 rectangles, 1¼" x 1½"

From the light plaid, cut:
1 square, 1½" x 1½"

FLYING X BLOCK

From a light print, cut:
4 squares, 1⅞" x 1⅞"; cut once diagonally to make
  8 triangles
4 squares, 1½" x 1½"

From the green prints, cut:
4 squares, 1⅞" x 1⅞"; cut once diagonally to make
  8 triangles

From a red print, cut:
4 squares, 1½" x 1½"

DIAMOND STAR BLOCK

From a light print, cut:
1 square, 3¼" x 3¼"; cut twice diagonally to make
  4 triangles
4 squares, 1½" x 1½"

From the red prints, cut:
4 squares, 1⅞" x 1⅞"; cut once diagonally to make
  8 triangles

From the green prints, cut:
4 squares, 1⅞" x 1⅞"; cut once diagonally to make
  8 triangles

DOUBLE FOUR PATCH BLOCK

From a light print, cut:
4 squares, 1½" x 1½"

From the red prints, cut:
4 squares, 1½" x 1½"

From a medium green print, cut:
2 squares, 2½" x 2½"

VERTICAL SASHING AND BINDING

From the dark brown print, cut:
4 strips, 1" x 20½"
4 binding strips, 1¾" x 20"

From the brown floral, cut:
1 strip, 2½" x 20½"

From the assorted brown prints, cut:
22 to 26 rectangles, 2½" x 1½" to 3¾" long

Making the Basket Block

1. Sew a red 1⅞" triangle and a light 1⅞" triangle together to make a half-square-triangle unit; press. Make five half-square-triangle units.

Make 5.

2. Sew the medium green 2⅞" triangles and the dark green 2⅞" triangles together to make a half-square-triangle unit. Press the seam allowances toward the dark green print.

3. Sew a dark green 1⅞" triangle to the end of a light rectangle as shown; press. Make a second unit, changing the orientation of the triangle.

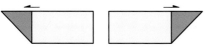

Make 1 of each.

4. Sew three red half-square-triangle units together as shown; press. Sew two red half-square-triangle units together, changing the orientation of the triangles.

Make 1 of each.

5. Arrange the units from steps 2–4 and the light 2⅞" triangle as shown. Sew the units together, adding the light triangle last; press in the direction of the arrows in the diagram, or press seam allowances open to reduce bulk.

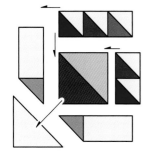
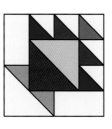

Making the Variable Star Block

1. Sew a green triangle to each short side of a light triangle to make a flying-geese unit; press. Make four flying-geese units.

Make 4.

2. Arrange the light squares, the flying-geese units, and the red center square as shown. Sew into rows; press. Sew the rows together to make the Variable Star block.

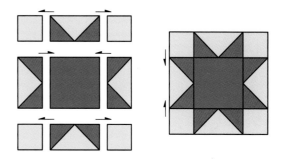

Making the Flock of Geese Block

1. Sew a light triangle to a red triangle to make a half-square-triangle unit; press. Make eight half-square-triangle units.

Make 8.

2. Sew a light plaid triangle to a dark green triangle to make a half-square-triangle unit; press. Make two half-square-triangle units.

3. Sew the red and light half-square-triangle units together in pairs as shown; press. Sew the pairs together. Make two units.

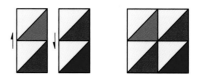

Make 2.

4. Arrange the units from steps 2 and 3 as shown. Sew the units into pairs; sew the pairs together to make the Flock of Geese block; press.

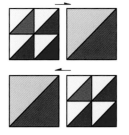 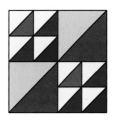

Making the Double X Block

1. Sew a light triangle to a green triangle to make a half-square-triangle unit. Make 10 half-square-triangle units.

Make 10.

2. Arrange the units from step 1, two light squares, and the red square in rows as shown. Sew the units into rows; sew the rows together to make a Double X block.

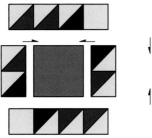 

Making the Buckeye Beauty Block

1. Sew a green triangle to a light triangle to make a half-square-triangle unit; press. Make two half-square-triangle units.

2. Sew the light squares and red squares together as shown to make two four-patch units.

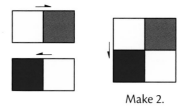

Make 2.

3. Sew the units from steps 1 and 2 together as shown to make the Buckeye Beauty block.

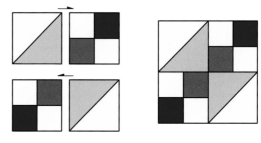

Making the Anvil Block

1. Sew a light 1⅞" triangle and a dark green 1⅞" triangle together to make a half-square-triangle unit; press. Make four half-square-triangle units.

Make 4.

2. Sew a light 2⅞" triangle and a red 2⅞" triangle together to make a half-square-triangle unit; press. Make two half-square-triangle units.

3. Arrange the units from steps 1 and 2 with the medium green and light squares as shown. Sew the squares and green half-square-triangle units together, and then sew the units together to make the Anvil block.

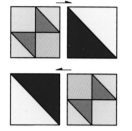

Making the Churn Dash Block

1. Sew a red triangle to a light triangle to make a half-square-triangle unit; press. Make four half-square-triangle units.

Make 4.

2. Sew a light rectangle to a dark green rectangle along their long sides; press. Make four units.

Make 4.

3. Arrange the units from steps 1 and 2 in rows with the light plaid square as shown. Sew the units into rows. Sew the rows together to make the Churn Dash block; press.

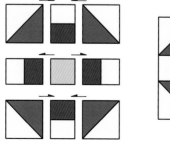

Making the Flying X Block

1. Sew a green triangle to a light triangle to make a half-square-triangle unit; press. Make eight half-square-triangle units.

Make 8.

2. Arrange the half-square-triangle units, the light squares, and the red squares as shown. Sew the units together in groups of four. Sew the four sections together to make the Flying X block.

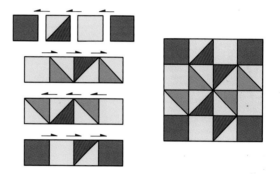

Making the Diamond Star Block

1. Sew a red triangle to a green triangle to make a half-square-triangle unit; press. Make four half-square-triangle units.

Make 4.

2. Sew a red triangle and a green triangle to the short sides of a light triangle as shown; press. Make four units.

Make 4.

3. Arrange the units from steps 1 and 2 as shown with the light squares. Sew the four half-square-triangle units in the center together; press. Sew the remaining units together in rows. Sew the rows together to make the Diamond Star block.

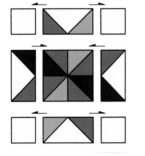 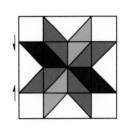

Making the Double Four Patch Block

1. Sew two light and two red squares together to make a four-patch unit. Make two.

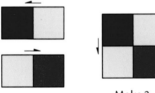

Make 2.

2. Sew the four-patch units to the medium green squares to make the Double Four Patch block.

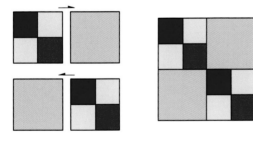

Assembling and Finishing the Quilt

1. Arrange the blocks into two vertical rows of five blocks each. Refer to the photograph for placement guidance, or arrange them as you prefer. Sew the blocks together into rows.

2. Sew the assorted brown rectangles together along the 2½" edges to make a pieced border strip that is at least 21" long; press. Trim the strip to 2½" x 20½". Repeat to make a second border strip.

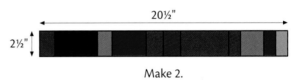

Make 2.

3. Referring to the quilt assembly diagram, sew a dark brown 1" x 20½" strip to one side of each pieced border strip; press.

4. Sew a dark brown 1" x 20½" strip to each side of the brown floral strip.

5. Arrange the rows as shown and sew them together; press.

6. Layer the quilt top, batting, and backing. Baste the layers together and quilt as desired. Add the binding and enjoy.

Vines and *Flowers*

Floral appliqué vines twisting along the diagonal paths created by the pieced blocks double the fun with the combination of machine piecing and appliqué. Select pale, muted tones for the Double X blocks to create an unexpected background for the appliqué.

Finished quilt: 16" x 20"
Finished Double X block: 4½" x 4½"

Materials

1 fat quarter or scraps of off-white prints for
    blocks
1 fat quarter of dark green print for bias vine
    and leaves
1 fat quarter of rose floral for border
1 fat quarter *total* of assorted scraps of 12 light
    to medium green prints for blocks and leaves
1 fat eighth *total* of assorted scraps of medium to
    dark red prints for flower appliqués
1 fat quarter of fabric for binding
1 fat quarter of fabric for backing
18" x 22" piece of batting

Cutting

From the off-white prints, cut *a total of*:
36 squares, 2⅜" x 2⅜"; cut once diagonally to
    make 72 triangles
24 squares, 2" x 2"

**From *each* of the 12 light to medium green
prints, cut:**
3 squares, 2⅜" x 2⅜"; cut once diagonally to
    make 6 triangles (72 total)
1 square, 2" x 2" (12 total)

From the dark green print, cut:
1¼"-wide bias strips to total 66"

From the rose floral, cut:
1 strip, 2½" x 14"
2 strips, 1¾" x 20½"

From the binding fabric, cut:
4 strips, 1¾" x 20"

Making the Double X Blocks

1. Sew an off-white 2⅜" triangle and a green 2⅜"
triangle together to make a half-square-triangle
unit. Make six for one block.

Make 6.

2. Arrange the units from step 1, two 2"
background squares, and one 2" matching green
square in rows as shown. Sew the units into rows;
sew the rows together to make a block. Repeat to
make a total of 12 blocks.

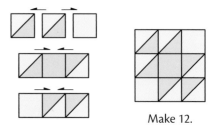

Make 12.

3. Arrange the blocks into four rows of three blocks
each. Sew the blocks into rows and sew the rows
together.

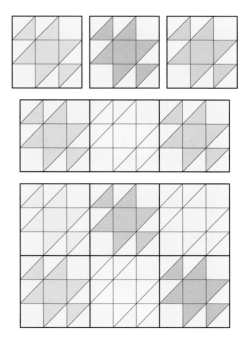

Appliquéing the Flowers and Vines

1. Draw lines freehand on your quilt top as shown for placement of the bias vines. Skip alternating diagonal rows, allowing each one to be different. This will give a casual and natural appearance to your vines.

2. Prepare the vines using the green bias strips. Pin or baste the vines in position and appliqué them in place on the quilt top.

3. Prepare the appliqué pieces for the flowers and leaves, referring to "Needle-Turn Hand Appliqué" on page 90 or using your favorite technique. Cut some of the leaves slightly different for variety and a natural look.

4. Arrange the leaves along the vines, adding or subtracting flowers and leaves as desired. When you are pleased with the arrangement, appliqué the pieces in place. Press the quilt top after the appliqué is complete.

> Patterns do not include seam allowances.

5. Sew the rose floral 2½" x 14" strip to the bottom of the quilt; press. Sew a rose floral 1¾" x 20½" strip to each side; press.

6. Layer the quilt top, batting, and backing. Baste the layers together and quilt as desired. Add the binding and enjoy.

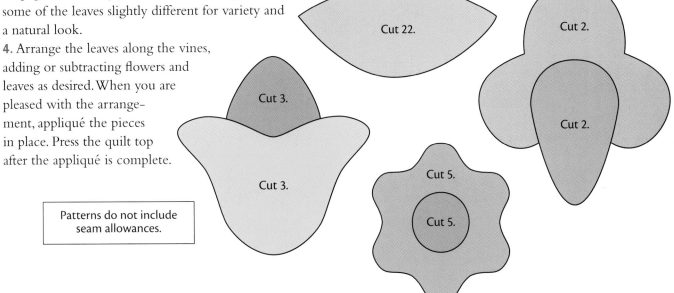

Cut 22.

Cut 2.

Cut 2.

Cut 3.

Cut 3.

Cut 5.

Cut 5.

Garden Path

Pairing appliqué with piecing creates a stunning combination in this traditionally inspired quilt. Framed within a pieced border, the simplified appliqué motifs add to the folk-art charm. The hand-quilted vine of leaves in the outer border repeats the garden-themed appliqué design.

Finished quilt: 16" x 20"
Finished Hourglass block: 2" x 2"

Materials

1 fat quarter of cheddar fabric for appliqué
    background and borders
1 fat quarter *total* of assorted medium-light to
    medium prints for appliqué and blocks
1 fat quarter *total* of assorted medium dark to
    dark prints for appliqué and blocks
1 fat quarter of fabric for binding
1 fat quarter of fabric for backing
18" x 22" piece of batting

Cutting

From the cheddar fabric, cut:
1 square, 9" x 9"
2 strips, 2½" x 12½"
2 strips, 2½" x 16½"

From the assorted medium-light to medium prints, cut:
18 squares, 3¼" x 3¼"; cut twice diagonally to
    make 72 triangles

From the assorted medium-dark to dark prints, cut:
18 squares, 3¼" x 3¼"; cut twice diagonally to
    make 72 triangles

From the binding fabric, cut:
4 strips, 1¾" x 20"

Appliquéing the Center

1. Referring to "Needle-Turn Hand Appliqué" on page 90, cut and prepare the appliqué pieces using the patterns on page 45. Cut the stems on the bias.

2. Fold and lightly press the cheddar 9" background square in fourths to find the center.

3. Align the dashed lines on the appliqué pattern with the creases in the background fabric. Mark the appliqué pattern on the background fabric.

4. Arrange the appliqué pieces on the background and appliqué them in place using your favorite method.

5. Press the appliquéd quilt center from the wrong side and trim to 8½" x 8½", centering the design.

Making the Hourglass Blocks and Border

1. Sew together two medium-light to medium and two medium-dark to dark triangles as shown to make the Hourglass block; press. Make 36 Hourglass blocks.

Make 36.

2. Sew four Hourglass blocks together; press. Make two of these strips for the side borders. Sew six Hourglass blocks together for the top and bottom; press. Repeat to make four of these strips.

Make 2.

Make 4.

3. Sew the shorter strips from step 2 to the sides of the appliquéd quilt center; press. Sew the longer strips from step 2 to the top and bottom; press. Sew a second border strip to the top and bottom.

Assembling and Finishing the Quilt

1. Sew the cheddar 2½" x 16½" strips to the sides of the quilt; press.

2. Sew an Hourglass block to each end of the remaining two cheddar border strips. Sew them to the top and bottom of the quilt.

3. Layer the quilt top, batting, and backing. Baste the layers together and quilt as desired. Add the binding and enjoy.

Patterns do not include
seam allowances.

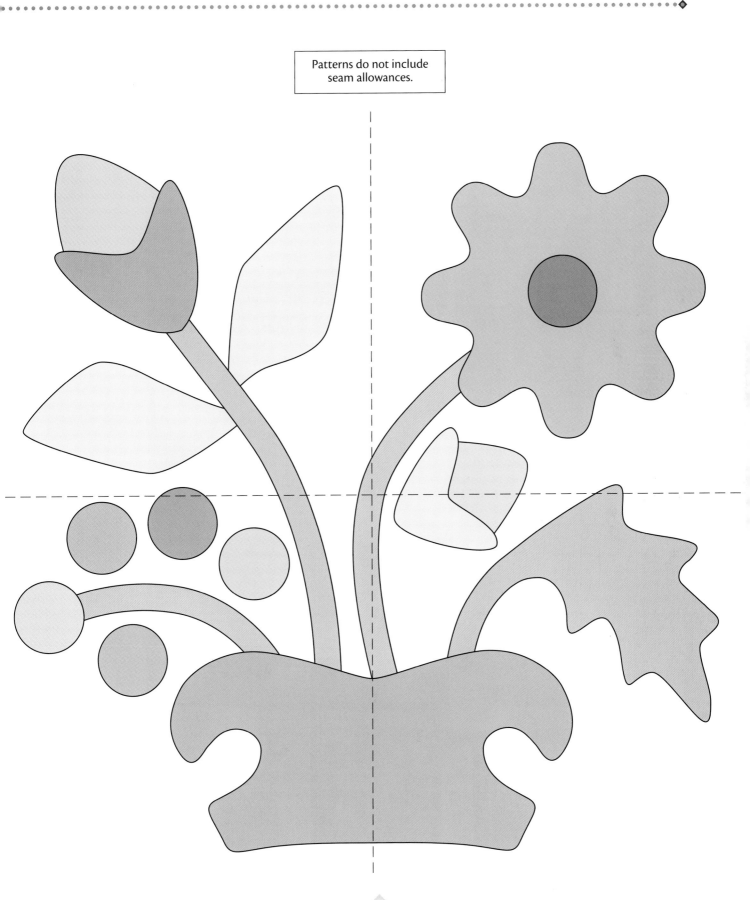

Square Dance

Here's your chance to highlight a collection of reproduction fabrics using both machine piecing and appliqué. The warm colors and visual movement in this quilt bring to mind an outdoor dance on a summer evening.

Finished quilt: 16" x 20"
Finished block: 3½" x 3½"

Materials

2 fat quarters *total* of assorted scraps in various colors and prints for blocks and appliqués
1 fat quarter of dark brown print for border
1 fat eighth of green print for bias vine
1 fat quarter of fabric for binding
1 fat quarter of fabric for backing
18" x 22" piece of batting

Cutting

Each block is made from 4 different print fabrics. Cut the pieces as indicated for each block. Repeat the cutting to make 12 blocks, keeping the fabrics for each block separate. For a paper-piecing option, cut the pieces oversized as noted, and make 12 copies of the pattern on page 48.

FOR ONE BLOCK
From print 1, cut:
1 square, 1¾" x 1¾"★

From print 2, cut:
2 squares, 1¾" x 1¾"; cut once diagonally to make 4 triangles★

From print 3, cut:
2 squares, 2⅛" x 2⅛"; cut once diagonally to make 4 triangles★★

From print 4, cut:
2 squares, 2⅝" x 2⅝"; cut once diagonally to make 4 triangles†

FOR BORDERS AND BINDING
From the fat quarter of dark brown print, cut:
2 strips, 3¼" x 14½"
2 strips, 3½" x 16½"

From the fat eighth of green print, cut:
1¼"-wide bias strips to total 45"

From the binding fabric, cut:
4 strips, 1¾" x 20"

★*Cut these squares 2¼" for paper piecing.*
★★*Cut these squares 2¾" for paper piecing.*
†*Cut these squares 3¼" for paper piecing.*

Making the Blocks

1. Sew the four print 2 triangles to the sides of the print 1 square; press.

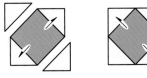

2. Sew four print 3 triangles to the sides of the unit from step 1; press.

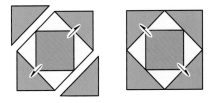

3. Sew the four print 4 triangles to the sides of the unit from step 2; press. The block should measure 4" x 4".

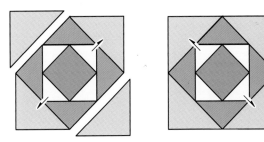

4. Repeat steps 1–3 to make a total of 12 blocks.

Assembling the Quilt and Adding the Appliqué

1. Arrange the blocks in four horizontal rows of three blocks each. Sew the blocks into rows using a shortened stitch length. Press the seam allowances open. Sew the rows together and press the seam allowances open.

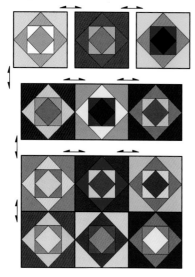

2. Sew the dark brown 3¼" x 14½" border strips to the sides of the quilt; press. Sew the dark brown 3½" x 16½" border strips to the top and bottom; press.

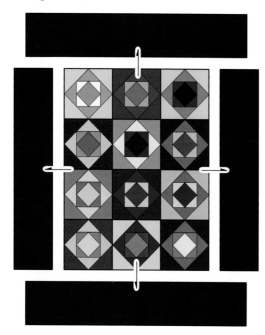

3. Referring to "Needle-Turn Hand Appliqué" on page 90, cut and prepare the appliqué pieces using the patterns on pages 49–51. Prepare the green 1¼" bias strips as instructed on page 90.

4. Arrange the appliqué pieces on the borders using the photo on page 46 as a placement guide. Fold the top and bottom borders in half and mark a crease to center the heart and flowerpot. The base of the flowerpot will extend into the seam allowance.

5. Appliqué the pieces in place.

6. Layer the quilt top, batting, and backing. Baste the layers together and quilt as desired. Add the binding and enjoy.

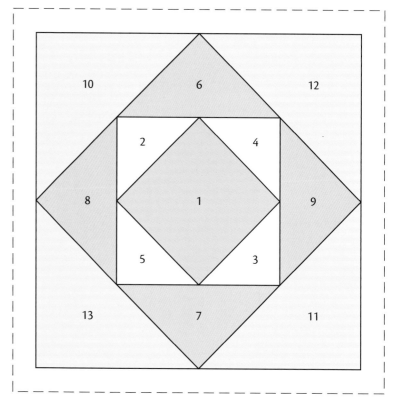

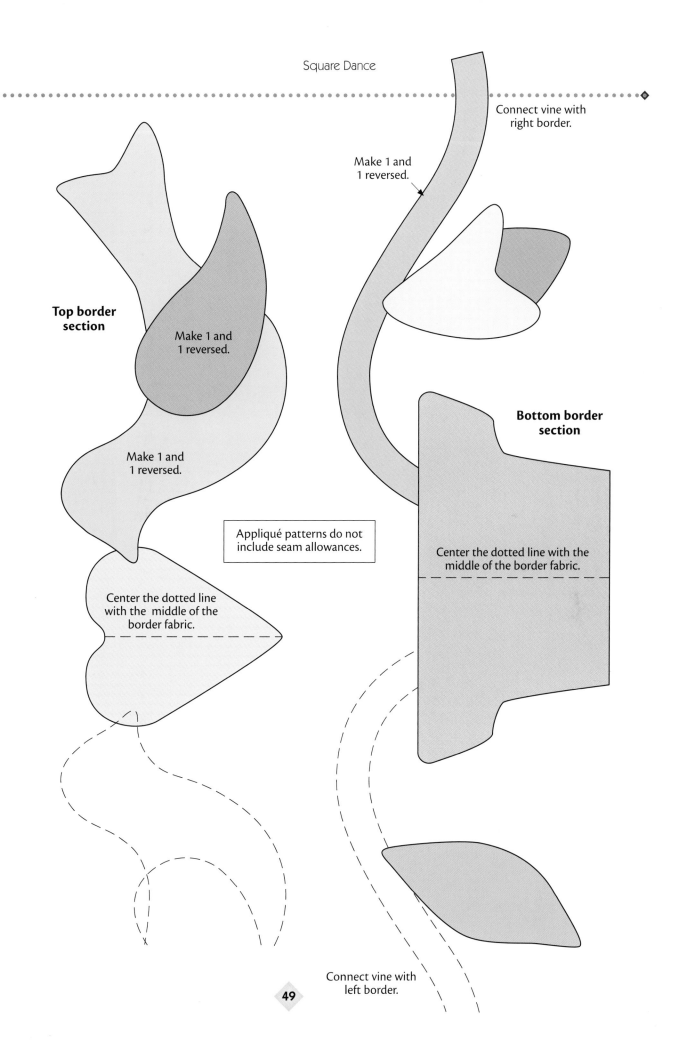

Connect vine with
right border.

Make 1 and
1 reversed.

**Top border
section**

Make 1 and
1 reversed.

Make 1 and
1 reversed.

**Bottom border
section**

Appliqué patterns do not
include seam allowances.

Center the dotted line with the
middle of the border fabric.

Center the dotted line
with the middle of the
border fabric.

Connect vine with
left border.

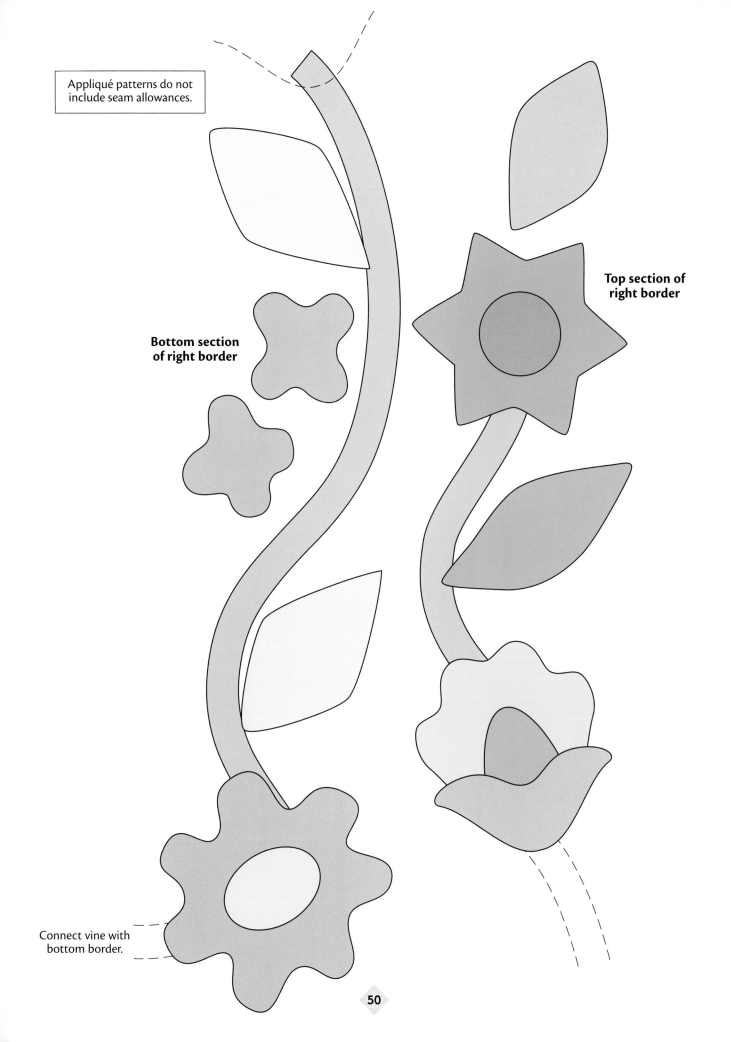

Appliqué patterns do not include seam allowances.

Top section of right border

Bottom section of right border

Connect vine with bottom border.

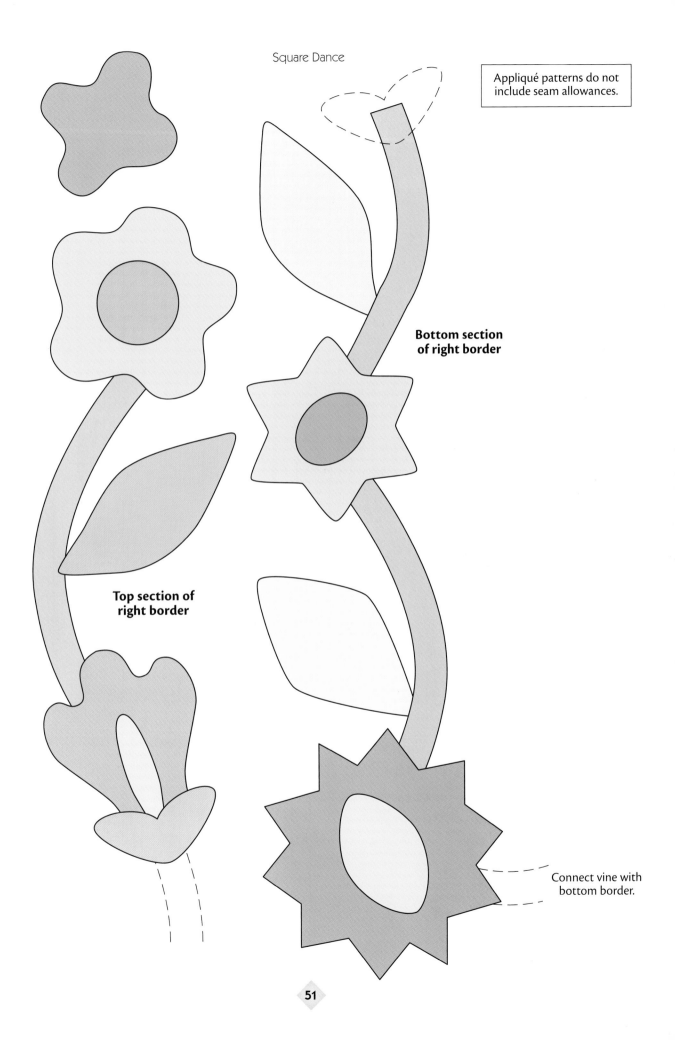

Appliqué patterns do not
include seam allowances.

Bottom section
of right border

Top section of
right border

Connect vine with
bottom border.

51

Simply Charming

This medallion-style quilt is simply charming and a joy to make from start to finish! Create it from a variety of colors and prints for maximum appeal. Maybe you'll even use up some of your scraps!

Finished quilt: 16" x 20"

Materials

1 fat quarter of light print for appliqué
  background
1 fat quarter of brown striped fabric for
  middle border
1 fat eighth of gold print for inner border
1 fat quarter *total* of assorted light to medium
  prints for pieced border
1 fat quarter *total* of assorted medium and
  dark prints for pieced border and appliqués
Scrap (6" x 6") of red print for border corner
  squares
Scrap (5" x 5") of rose print for border corner
  squares and appliqués
Scrap (4" x 4") of dark brown print for border
  corner squares
1 fat quarter of fabric for binding
1 fat quarter of fabric for backing
18" x 22" piece of batting

Cutting

From the fat quarter of light print, cut:
1 rectangle, 8½" x 12½"

From the fat eighth of gold print, cut:
2 strips, 1¼" x 8"
2 strips, 1¼" x 12"

From the scrap of dark brown print, cut:
4 squares, 1¼" x 1¼"

From the fat quarter of brown striped fabric, cut:
2 strips, 2" x 9½"
2 strips, 2" x 13½"

From the scrap of rose print, cut:
4 squares, 2" x 2"

From the fat quarter of assorted medium and dark prints, cut:
14 squares, 2⅞" x 2⅞"; cut once diagonally to
  yield 28 triangles

From the fat quarter of assorted light to medium prints, cut:
14 squares, 2⅞" x 2⅞"; cut once diagonally to
  yield 28 triangles

From the scrap of red print, cut:
4 squares, 2½" x 2½"

From the binding fabric, cut:
4 strips, 1¾" x 20"

Appliquéing the Center

1. Referring to "Needle-Turn Hand Appliqué" on page 90, cut and prepare the appliqué pieces using the patterns on page 55. Cut the stems on the bias.
2. Fold and lightly press the light 8½" x 12½" background rectangle in fourths.
3. Align the dashed lines on the appliqué pattern with the creases in the background fabric. Mark the appliqué pattern on the background fabric.
4. Arrange the appliqué pieces on the background and appliqué them in place using your favorite method.

5. Press the appliquéd quilt center from the wrong side and trim to 8" x 12", centering the design.

Assembling the Quilt

1. Referring to the assembly diagram at right, sew the gold 1¼" x 12" strips to the sides of the appliquéd quilt center. Sew a dark brown 1¼" square to each end of the gold 1¼" x 8" strips and sew the strips to the top and bottom.

2. Sew the brown striped 2" x 13½" strips to the sides. Sew a rose 2" square to each end of the remaining brown striped strips and sew the strips to the top and bottom.

3. Sew light and medium print triangles to medium and dark print triangles to make 28 half-square-triangle units. Press seam allowances toward the darker triangles.

Make 28.

4. Arrange the half-square-triangle units around the center of the quilt, placing the base of the darker triangles next to the quilt center. Sew eight units together for each side border.

5. Sew six half-square-triangle units together for the top and bottom borders, adding a red 2½" square to each end.

6. Sew the pieced borders from step 4 to the sides of the quilt; press. Sew the pieced borders from step 5 to the top and bottom of the quilt; press.

7. Layer the quilt top, batting, and backing. Baste the layers together and quilt as desired. Add the binding and enjoy.

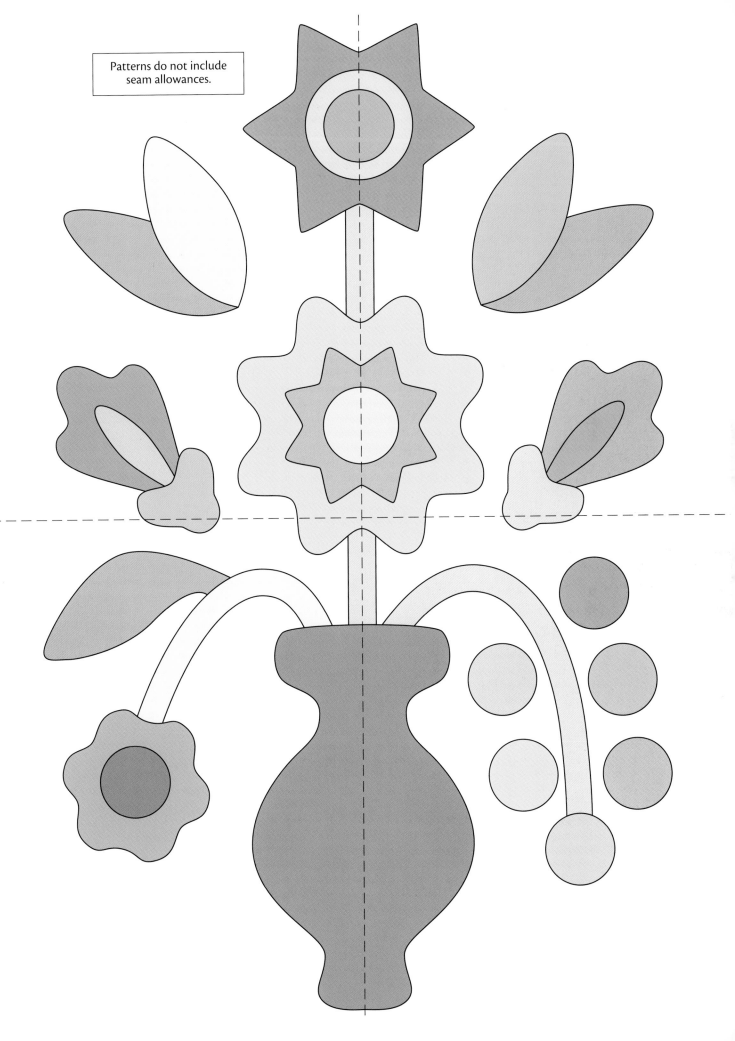

Patterns do not include seam allowances.

Baskets, 1930s Style

If you love the reproduction prints and colors reminiscent of the 1930s, here's the quilt for you! Listen to the birds sing and imagine yourself gathering baskets full of berries from the garden as you cut and stitch with your favorite prints.

Finished quilt: 16" x 20"
Finished block: 4" x 4"

Materials

2 fat quarters of muslin or white fabric for
   blocks and border
2 fat quarters *total* of assorted scraps of '30s
   reproduction prints in pink, lavender,
   blue, yellow, and green for blocks, setting
   triangles, and appliqués
1 fat quarter of green '30s reproduction print
   for bias vines
1 fat quarter of fabric for binding
1 fat quarter of fabric for backing
18" x 22" piece of batting

Cutting

*Each block is made from 3 to 5 different print fabrics
of the same color.*

**From the scraps of *each of 8* assorted '30s
reproduction prints, cut:**
3 squares, 1⅞" x 1⅞"; cut once diagonally to make
   6 triangles (48 total)
1 square, 2⅞" x 2⅞"; cut once diagonally to make
   2 triangles (16 total; use 8 for the pieced setting
   triangles)

**From the remaining assorted '30s
reproduction prints, cut a total of:**
12 squares, 2⅞" x 2⅞"; cut once diagonally to
   make 24 triangles

From the muslin or white fabric, cut:
16 squares, 1⅞" x 1⅞"; cut once diagonally to
   make 32 triangles
8 squares, 2⅞" x 2⅞"; cut once diagonally to
   make 16 triangles
8 squares, 1½" x 1½"
16 rectangles, 1½" x 2½"
2 strips, 2⅞" x 17½"
1 strip, 3½" x 16½"

**From the fat quarter of green '30s
reproduction print, cut:**
1"-wide bias strips to total 68"

From the binding fabric, cut:
4 strips, 1¾" x 20"

Making the Blocks

1. Sew a muslin 2⅞" triangle to a lavender 2⅞"
triangle to make a half-square-triangle unit. Press
the seam allowances toward the lavender print.

2. Sew four muslin 1⅞" triangles and four lavender
1⅞" triangles together in two separate units as
shown; press. Add a muslin 1½" square to one of
the units.

Make 1 of each.

3. Sew a lavender 1⅞" triangle to the end of a
muslin 1½" x 2½" rectangle; press. Make a second
unit, changing the orientation of the triangle.

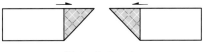

Make 1 of each.

4. Sew the units from step 2 to the unit from step
1; press. Add the units from step 3, and then add
the muslin 2⅞" triangle to the corner; press in the
direction of the arrows in the diagram, or press seam
allowances open to reduce bulk. The block should
measure 4½" x 4½".

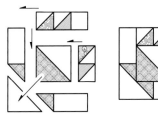

5. Repeat steps 1–4 to make a total of eight blocks in assorted colors.

Assembling the Quilt

1. Sew assorted 2⅞" triangles together in units of four and two as shown. These will be the side setting triangles and corner setting triangles. Make six side setting triangles and four corner setting triangles. Handle them carefully, as the edges will be bias.

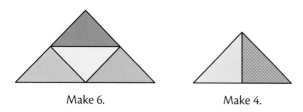

Make 6.   Make 4.

2. Arrange the Basket blocks and units from step 1 together in diagonal rows. Rotate the Basket blocks so that the two at the top and the two at the bottom are horizontal. Sew the blocks and triangle units into rows; press. Sew the rows together to make the quilt top. Press in the direction of the arrows, or press seam allowances open if desired to reduce bulk.

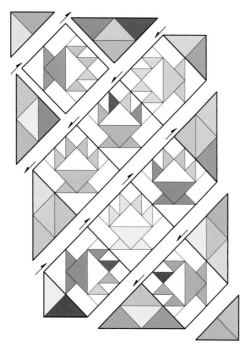

3. Sew the muslin 2⅞" x 17½" border strips to the sides; press. Sew the muslin 3½" x 16½" strip to the bottom; press.

4. Referring to "Needle-Turn Hand Appliqué" on page 90, cut and prepare the appliqué pieces using the patterns on page 59.

5. Draw the curve for the vine on the side borders. Center the flowerpot in the bottom border and draw the vines coming out of the flowerpot on either side.

6. Arrange and pin the appliqué pieces on the border backgrounds. Refer to the photograph on page 56 for placement guidance. Appliqué the pieces in place using your favorite method.

7. Layer the quilt top, batting, and backing. Baste the layers together and quilt as desired. Add the binding and enjoy.

Patterns do not include
seam allowances.

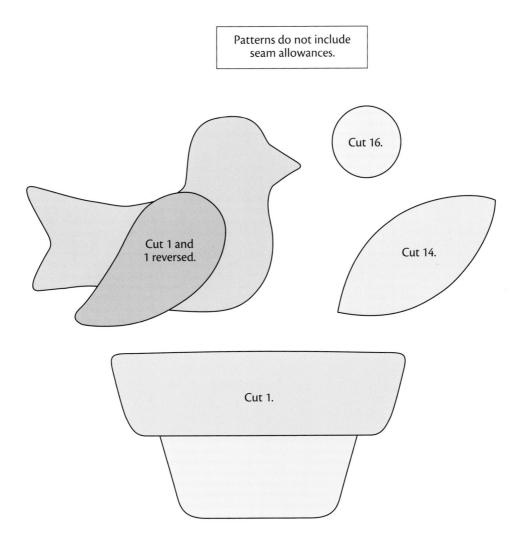

Cut 16.

Cut 14.

Cut 1 and
1 reversed.

Cut 1.

Pinwheels in My Garden

Pinks, browns, and creams were used to create a medallion-style quilt that again combines my love of appliqué with machine piecing. The stylized petals within the appliqué flowers echo the shapes of the Pinwheel blocks while the alternating blocks within the border create diamond shapes to highlight the Pinwheels. Select a variety of values of pink and brown prints to add contrast to the limited color scheme.

Finished quilt: 16" x 20"
Finished appliquéd block: 8" x 12"
Finished Pinwheel and Hourglass
    blocks: 2" x 2"

Materials

1 fat quarter of cream print for appliqué
    background
3 fat eighths *total* of assorted pink prints for
    blocks and appliqués
3 fat eighths *total* of assorted brown prints for
    blocks and appliqués
1 fat quarter *total* of assorted cream prints for
    blocks
1 fat quarter of fabric for binding
1 fat quarter of fabric for backing
18" x 22" piece of batting

Cutting

From the fat quarter of cream print, cut:
1 rectangle, 9" x 13"

From the assorted brown prints, cut:
14 squares, 1⅞" x 1⅞"; cut once diagonally to
    make 28 triangles★
14 squares, 3¼" x 3¼"; cut twice diagonally to
    make 56 triangles

From the assorted cream prints, cut:
28 squares, 1⅞" x 1⅞"; cut once diagonally to
    make 56 triangles★

From the assorted pink prints, cut:
14 squares, 1⅞" x 1⅞"; cut once diagonally to
    make 28 triangles★
14 squares, 3¼" x 3¼"; cut twice diagonally to
    make 56 triangles

From the binding fabric, cut:
4 strips, 1¾" x 20"

★*Cut in matching pairs for Pinwheel blocks
with coordinating fabrics.*

Appliquéing the Center Block

1. Referring to "Needle-Turn Hand Appliqué"
on page 90, cut and prepare the appliqué pieces
using the patterns on page 63. Enlarge the pattern
125%. Cut the stems on the bias, adding a ³⁄₁₆" seam
allowance for hand appliqué.
2. Fold and lightly press the cream 9" x 13" background rectangle in fourths.
3. Align the dashed lines on the appliqué pattern
with the creases in the background fabric. Mark the
appliqué pattern on the background fabric.
4. Arrange the appliqué pieces on the background;
pin and appliqué them in place using your favorite
method.

5. Press the appliquéd quilt center from the wrong
side and trim to 8½" x 12½", centering the design.

Piecing the Border Blocks

1. Select four matching pink 1⅞" triangles and four
matching cream 1⅞" triangles for each Pinwheel
block. Sew a pink and a cream triangle together
to make a half-square-triangle unit. Make four.
Sew the units together in rows, and then sew the
rows together to make the Pinwheel blocks. Make
14 pink-and-cream Pinwheel blocks. The blocks
should measure 2½" x 2½".

Make 14.

2. Select four brown 1⅞" triangles and four cream 1⅞" triangles for each Pinwheel block. Repeat step 1 to make 14 brown-and-cream Pinwheel blocks.

Make 14.

3. Working on a design wall, arrange the Pinwheel blocks around the appliquéd quilt center, leaving space for the Hourglass blocks, which will be sewn in step 6. Refer to the quilt diagram below and the quilt photograph on page 60.

4. Place pink 3¼" triangles around the pink Pinwheel blocks. Most of the Pinwheel blocks require three triangles from the same pink fabric around them. Use the remaining pink triangles along the outer and inner edges of the pieced border where only one triangle is required.

5. Repeat step 4 to place the brown 3¼" triangles around the brown Pinwheel blocks.

6. Sew the quarter-square triangles together as shown to make the Hourglass blocks. Make sure that you keep the fabrics in the correct position

in each block. The blocks should measure 2½" x 2½". Make 28.

Make 28.

7. Place the Hourglass blocks back on the design wall. Then sew the blocks together in rows. Press the seam allowances open to eliminate bulk.

8. Sew the border rows together and press seam allowances open.

9. Sew the side rows to the appliqué block; press. Sew the top and bottom rows to the quilt.

10. Layer the quilt top, batting, and backing. Baste the layers together and quilt as desired. Add the binding and enjoy.

Stitch Length for Pressing Open

When working with small blocks, pressing the seam allowances open helps to distribute the fabric in the seams and produces sharper points along the edges of the blocks. When pressing seam allowances open, sew with a shorter stitch length to strengthen the seams and prevent any migration of batting through the seams.

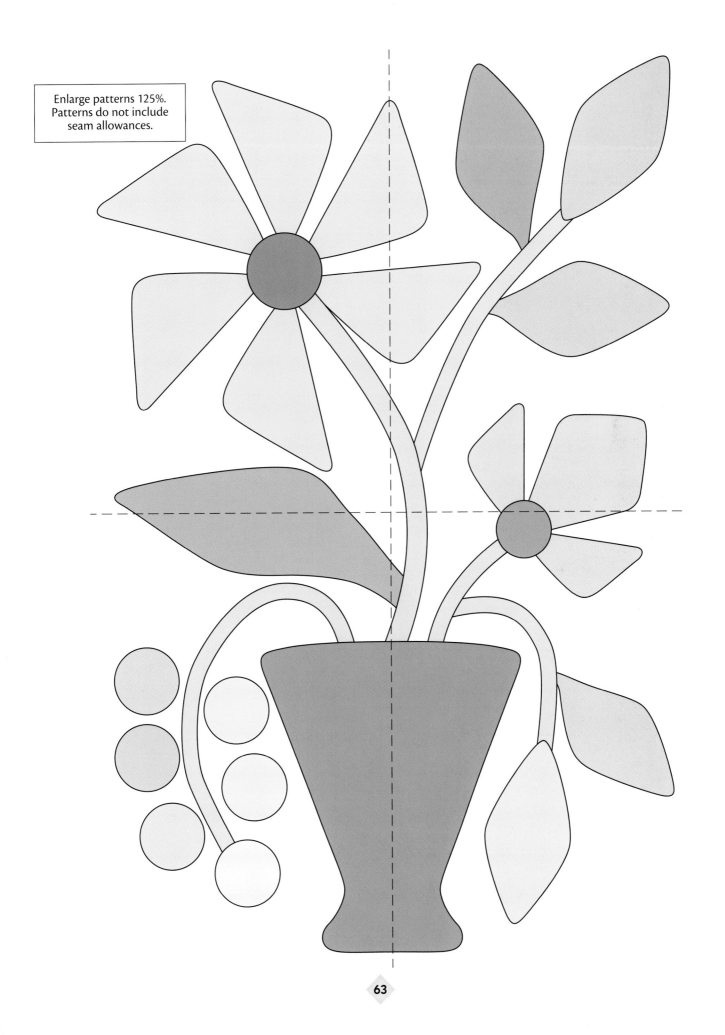

Enlarge patterns 125%.
Patterns do not include
seam allowances.

Birds in the Air

Colors typical of quilts from the mid-1800s add drama and excitement to this quilt. Reminiscent of quilts of yesteryear, the stylized appliqué motifs fill the quilt center along with the significant date appliquéd in the corner. Finish the quilt with a pieced border and hand quilt with zigzag lines freehand quilted across the entire surface of the quilt.

Finished quilt: 16" x 20"

Materials

1 fat quarter and 1 fat eighth of light print for
  appliqué background and border
1 fat quarter of red print for border and
  appliqués
1 fat quarter of green print for appliqués
1 fat eighth of gold print for appliqués
1 fat quarter of fabric for binding
1 fat quarter of fabric for backing
18" x 22" piece of batting

Cutting

From the light print, cut:
1 rectangle, 14" x 20½"
16 squares, 2⅛" x 2⅛"; cut once diagonally
  to make 32 triangles

From the red print, cut:
16 squares, 2⅛" x 2⅛"; cut once diagonally to
  make 32 triangles

From the binding fabric, cut:
4 strips, 1¾" x 20"

Appliquéing the Quilt

1. Referring to "Needle-Turn Hand Appliqué" on
page 90, cut and prepare the appliqué pieces using
the patterns on pages 66 and 67.
2. Fold and lightly press the light 14" x 20½"
background rectangle in fourths.
3. Center and position the appliqué designs,
referring to the placement guide (see assembly
diagram at right). Mark the appliqué pattern on the
background fabric.
4. Pin the appliqué pieces on the background and
appliqué them in place using your favorite method.
5. Press the appliquéd quilt center from the wrong
side.

Assembling and Finishing the Quilt

1. Sew a red triangle to a light triangle to make
a half-square-triangle unit. Make 32 half-square-
triangle units. They should measure 1¾" x 1¾".

Make 32.

2. Sew 16 of the half-square-triangle units together
as shown to make a side border. Make two side
borders.

Make 2.

3. Sew the pieced side borders to the sides of the
quilt; press.

4. Layer the quilt top, batting, and backing. Baste
the layers together and quilt as desired. Add the
binding and enjoy.

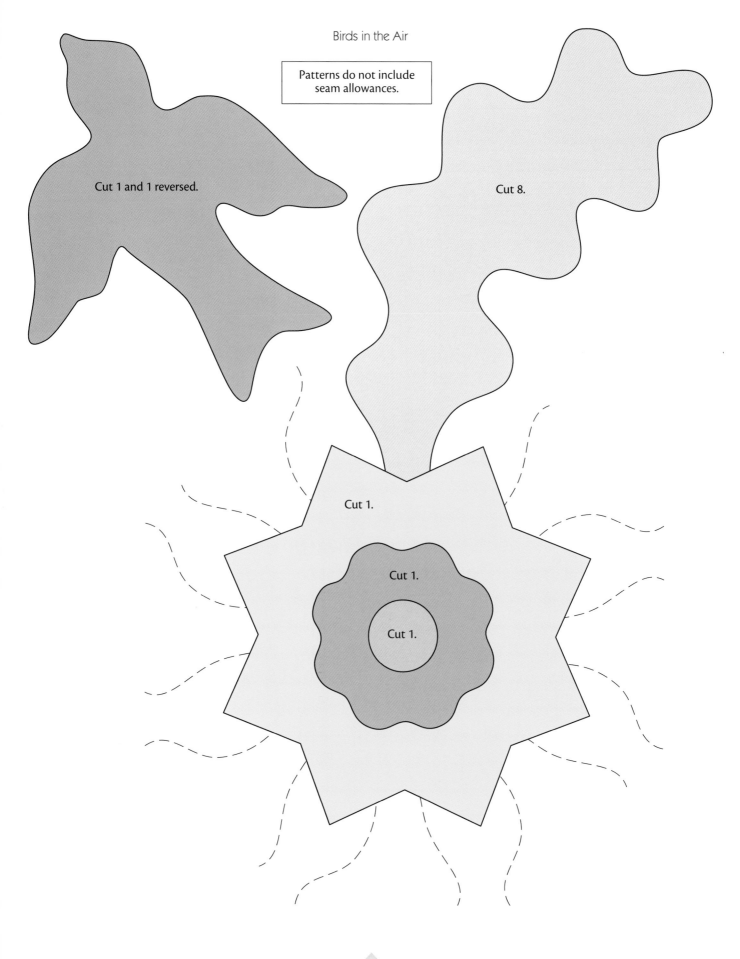

Birds in the Air

Patterns do not include
seam allowances.

Cut 1 and 1 reversed.

Cut 8.

Cut 1.

Cut 1.

Cut 1.

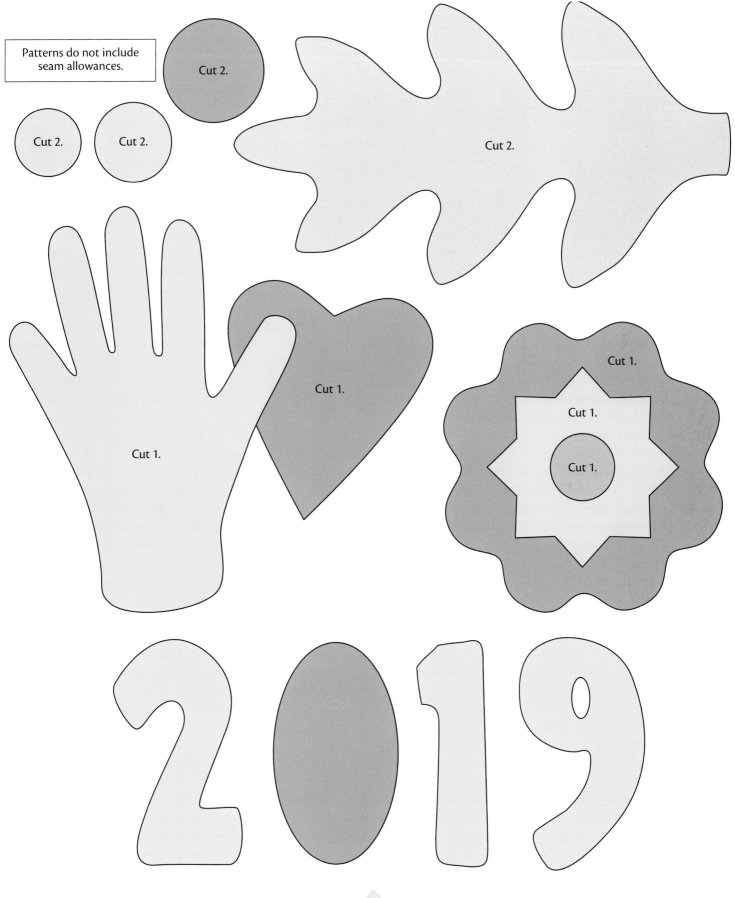

Patterns do not include seam allowances.

Cut 2.

Cut 2.

Cut 2.

Cut 2.

Cut 1.

Cut 1.

Cut 1.

Cut 1.

Cut 1.

Tumbling Leaves

Autumn is in the air with the geese flying south and vibrant leaves tumbling to the ground. An abundant crop awaits harvesting. Enjoy the crisp air and stitch up a small quilt to welcome the season.

Finished quilt: 16" x 20"
Finished block: 4½" x 4½"

Materials

8 fat eighths of assorted brown, orange, yellow, and green prints for blocks and appliqués
1 fat quarter of brown print for blocks and border
1 fat quarter of off-white print for block backgrounds
1 fat quarter of fabric for binding
1 fat quarter of fabric for backing
18" x 22" piece of batting

Cutting

From the fat quarter of off-white print, cut:
18 squares, 2" x 2"
27 squares, 2⅜" x 2⅜"; cut once diagonally to make 54 triangles

From *each* of the 8 fat eighths of assorted brown, orange, yellow, and green prints, cut:
2 squares, 2⅜" x 2⅜"; cut once diagonally to make 4 triangles (32 total)
3 squares, 2" x 2" (24 total)
1 bias strip, ¾" x 3" (8 total)

From the fat quarter of brown print, cut:
2 squares, 2⅜" x 2⅜"; cut once diagonally to make 4 triangles
3 squares, 2" x 2"
1 bias strip, ¾" x 3"
1 strip, 3" x 20½"
1 strip, 4" x 14"

From the leftovers of the 8 fat eighths of assorted brown, orange, yellow, and green prints, cut *a total of*:
3 squares, 4¼" x 4¼"; cut twice diagonally to make 12 triangles (1 is extra)

From the binding fabric, cut:
4 strips, 1¾" x 20"

Making the Blocks

1. Choose four 2⅜" triangles, three 2" squares, and one 3" bias strip of the same assorted print fabric. Sew the assorted triangles to the off-white triangles to make four half-square-triangle units.

2. Referring to "Needle-Turn Hand Appliqué" on page 90, appliqué the bias strip to one off-white 2" square along the diagonal as shown to make the stem. Trim the ends even with the square.

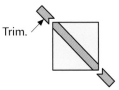

Trim.

3. Arrange the units from step 1, the three 2" squares, the appliquéd stem block, and an off-white 2" square in three horizontal rows as shown to make the Maple Leaf block. Sew the units into rows; press. Sew the rows together. The block should measure 5" x 5".

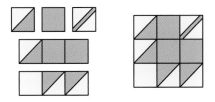

4. Repeat steps 1–3 using the pieces cut from the assorted fat eighths and the brown fat quarter to make a total of nine Maple Leaf blocks.

Assembling and Finishing the Quilt

1. Sew an off-white 2⅜" triangle to each side of an assorted 4¼" triangle as shown to make a flying-geese unit. Repeat to make nine flying-geese units, and then sew them together to make a row.

Make 9.

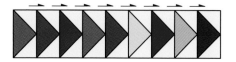

2. Arrange the Maple Leaf blocks in three horizontal rows of three blocks each. Position them in alternate directions as shown. Sew the blocks into rows and sew the rows together. Sew the flying-geese row to the top of the quilt.

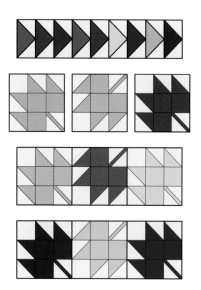

3. Sew the brown 4" x 14" border strip to the bottom of the quilt; press. Sew the brown 3" x 20½" border strip to the left side; press.

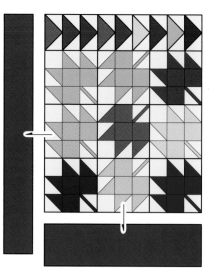

4. Referring to "Needle-Turn Hand Appliqué" on page 90, prepare the pumpkin and sunflower appliqués using the patterns on page 71. Cut the sunflower stem on the bias wide enough that it will finish ⅝" wide. Arrange the pieces on the quilt and appliqué them in place using your favorite method. Appliqué two assorted triangles in the upper-left corner.

5. Layer the quilt top, batting, and backing. Baste the layers together and quilt as desired. Add the binding and enjoy.

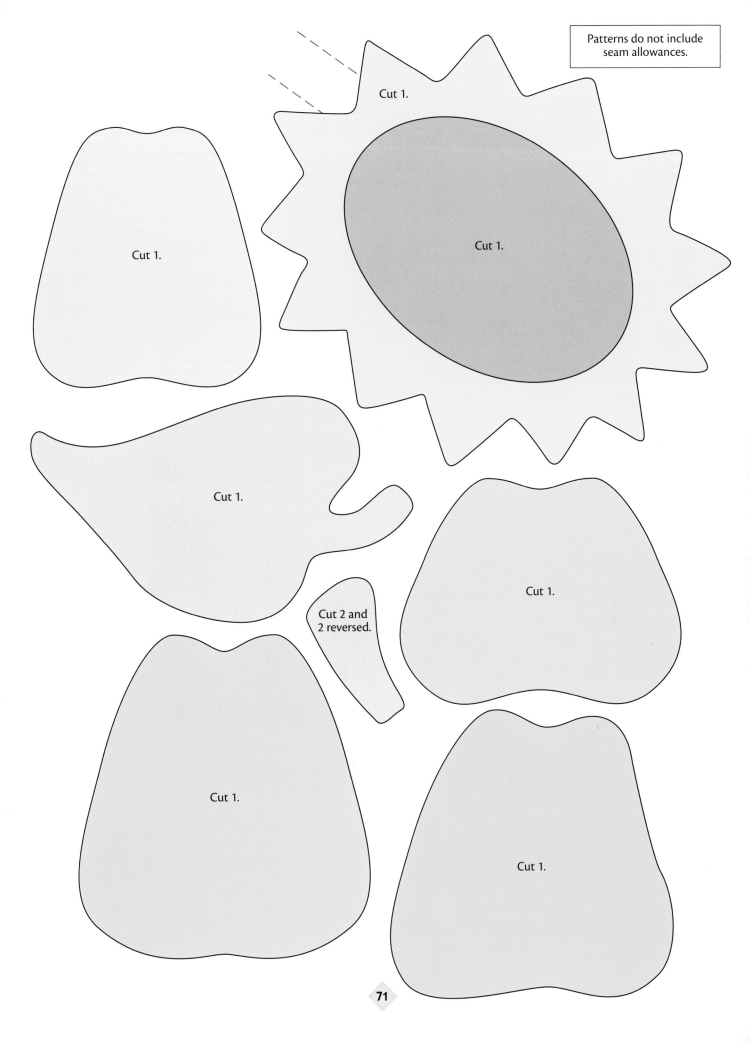

Cut 1.

Patterns do not include
seam allowances.

Cut 1.

Cut 1.

Cut 1.

Cut 2 and
2 reversed.

Cut 1.

Cut 1.

Cut 1.

Springtime Floral *Wreath*

Inspired by the colors within the floral border print, the soft pastel
appliqué blocks welcome a new beginning filled with hope and joy.
Create a quilted garden that is sure to warm the hearts of others.

Finished quilt: 16" x 20"

Materials

1 fat quarter of green floral for border
1 fat quarter of white print or solid for
    background
1 fat quarter of green print for stems, leaves,
    and binding
1 fat eighth of pink print for flowers and buds
3" x 20" piece of yellow print or solid for
    flower centers
1 fat quarter of fabric for backing
18" x 22" piece of batting

Cutting

From the green floral, cut:
1 strip, 2½" 12½"
2 strips, 2½" x 20½"

From the green print, cut:
4 strips, 1¾" x 20"

Appliquéing the Quilt

1. Using a marking pencil and referring to the
diagram shown top right, draw a grid of six 6" x 6"
squares on the background fabric.
2. Referring to "Needle-Turn Hand Appliqué" on
page 90, cut and prepare the appliqué pieces using
the patterns on page 74.
3. Arrange the appliqués within each 6" square and
appliqué in place using your favorite method.
4. Press the appliquéd panel from the wrong side and
trim to 12½" x 18½".

Assembling and Finishing the Quilt

1. Sew the floral 2½" x 12½" border strip to
the bottom of the quilt; press. Sew the floral
2½" x 20½" border strips to the sides; press.

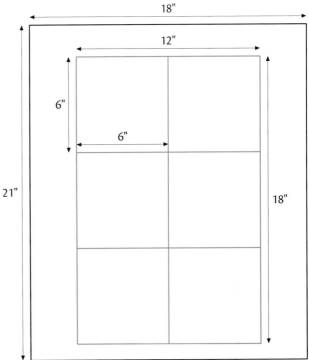

2. Layer the quilt top, batting, and backing. Baste
the layers together and quilt as desired. Stitch along
the marked grid lines to help define the "blocks."
Add the binding and enjoy.

Patterns do not include
seam allowances.

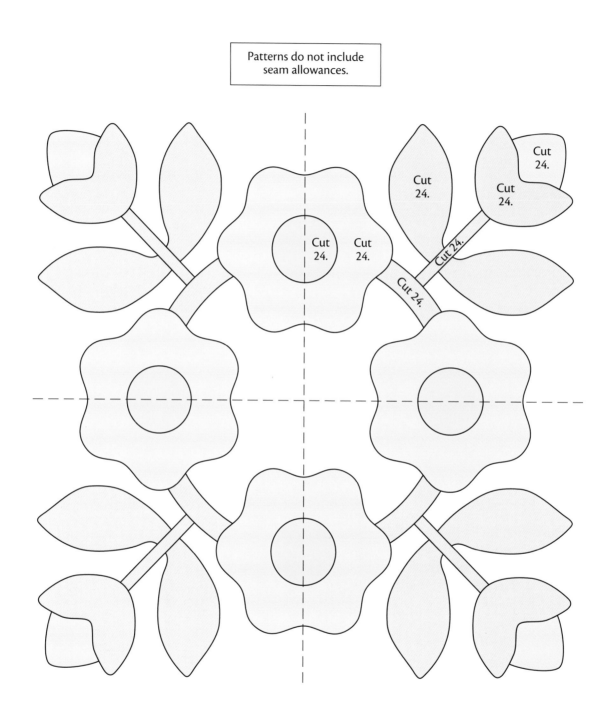

Dresden Plate Delight

Grandmother would be proud of this traditionally inspired Dresden Plate quilt done in 1930s reproduction fabrics. Surrounded by flowers, hearts, and a soft border print, it is sure to become a treasured family heirloom.

Finished quilt: 16" x 20"

Materials

1 fat quarter of muslin or off-white solid for
    background and circle appliqués
1 fat eighth of yellow print for borders
2 fat quarters *total* of assorted scraps of '30s
    reproduction prints in at least 8 different
    colors for appliqués
1 fat quarter of fabric for binding
1 fat quarter fabric for backing
18" x 22" piece of batting

Cutting

From the muslin or off-white fabric, cut:
1 strip, 2" x 21"

From the yellow print, cut:
2 strips, 1¾" x 20½"

From the binding fabric, cut:
4 strips, 1¾" x 20"

Appliquéing and Assembling the Quilt

1. Referring to "Needle-Turn Hand Appliqué"
on page 90, cut and prepare the appliqué pieces
for the flowers, leaves, and Dresden plates using
the patterns on page 77. Add a ¼" seam allowance
along the straight sides and the inside curve as
shown on the Dresden Plate pattern. Add a ³⁄₁₆"
seam allowance elsewhere for hand appliqué. Cut
a total of 64 wedge shapes from the assorted prints.
Cut eight circles from the muslin or off-white
2" x 21" strip. Cut six flowers and flower centers,
12 leaves, and four hearts.

2. Sew eight wedge shapes together by machine
along the straight edges using a ¼" seam allowance.
Trim the seam allowances to a generous ⅛" to
reduce bulk and press them open.

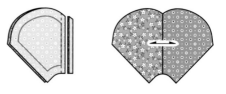

3. Appliqué the center circle in place. Repeat to
make eight Dresden-plate units.

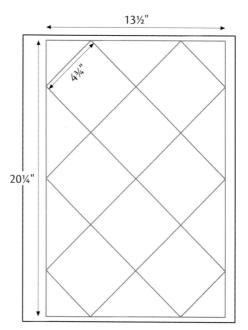

Make 8.

4. Use a marking pencil to draw a grid of 4¾"
squares on the remaining background fabric; it
should measure approximately 13½" x 20¼". Draw
the squares on point according to the diagram.

5. Arrange the Dresden-plate units, flowers, leaves, and hearts on the background fabric. Refer to the photograph on page 75 for placement guidance.

6. Appliqué the pieces in place on the background using your favorite method.

7. Press the appliquéd quilt center from the wrong side and trim to 14" x 20½".

8. Sew the yellow 1¾" x 20½" border strips to the sides of the quilt and press.

9. Layer the quilt top, batting, and backing. Baste the layers together and quilt as desired. Add the binding and enjoy.

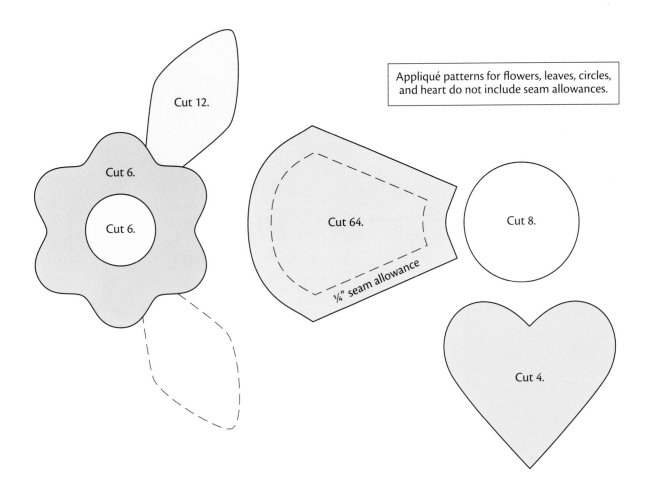

Appliqué patterns for flowers, leaves, circles, and heart do not include seam allowances.

Cut 12.

Cut 6.

Cut 6.

Cut 64.

¼" seam allowance

Cut 8.

Cut 4.

Whig Rose

Set on a dark background, the traditional Whig Rose appliqué
pattern reconnects us with our quilting heritage. This quilt is finished
with an appliquéd border framing two sides and quilted with zigzag
lines stitched freehand across the entire surface of the quilt.

Finished quilt: 16" x 20"

Materials

1 fat quarter of brown print for background
1 fat quarter of pale green print for appliqués
2 fat eighths of red prints for flowers and
   sawtooth border
1 fat eighth of green print for stems
1 fat eighth or scraps of cheddar print for
   flowers
1 fat quarter of fabric for binding
1 fat quarter of fabric for backing
18" x 22" piece of batting

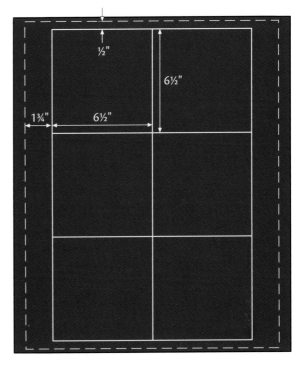

Cutting

From one red print, cut:
2 strips, 2" x 20½"

From the binding fabric, cut:
4 strips, 1¾" x 20"

Appliquéing the Quilt

The instructions are written for hand appliqué. You
can use your preferred method.

1. Use a marking pencil to draw a centered grid
of six 6½" squares on the right side of the brown
print fat quarter that will be your background.
Be sure that the markings can be easily removed
later. The background will be trimmed to 16½" x
20½" after the appliqué is complete, so be sure that
your fat quarter is at least 20½" wide. Also mark
the outer edges of the quilt as shown top right,
allowing 1¾" on each side and ½" along the top
and bottom.

2. Referring to "Needle-Turn Hand Appliqué" on
page 90, mark the placement of the appliqué pieces
on the background using the pattern on page 81.
3. Using your favorite method, prepare the
appliqué pieces and stitch them in place on each
square.
4. To add the sawtooth border, use the pattern
on page 80 as a guide for trimming the red
2" x 20½" strips. Roughly trace and repeat the
pattern across the length of the strips. Decide how
you want each end to appear and adjust the pattern
accordingly. Don't worry about being extremely
accurate or consistent when cutting. The folk-art
charm of this quilt is created in part by the casual
nature of the sawtooth border.
5. Cut the sawtooth border, adding a ³⁄₁₆" seam
allowance for hand appliqué.

6. Position the sawtooth borders on the quilt, aligning the straight raw edges with the outer lines that you drew in step 1. Pin the sawtooth border in place and baste the outer raw edges to the background. Appliqué the sawtooth edges.

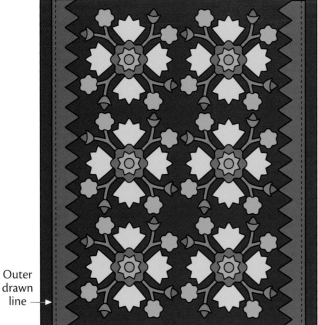

Outer drawn line →

Baste.

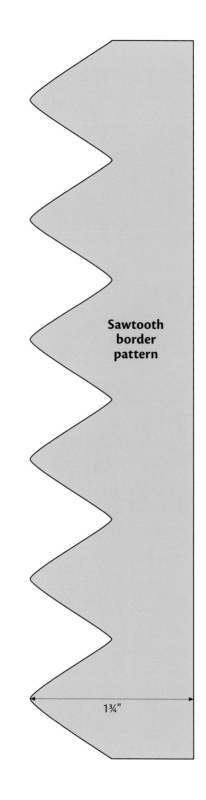

Sawtooth border pattern

1¾"

7. Press the appliquéd quilt center from the wrong side and trim it to 16½" x 20½".

8. Layer the quilt top, batting, and backing. Baste the layers together and quilt as desired. Add a line of quilting along the grid lines that you drew to make the "blocks" stand out. Add the binding and enjoy.

Patterns do not include
seam allowances.

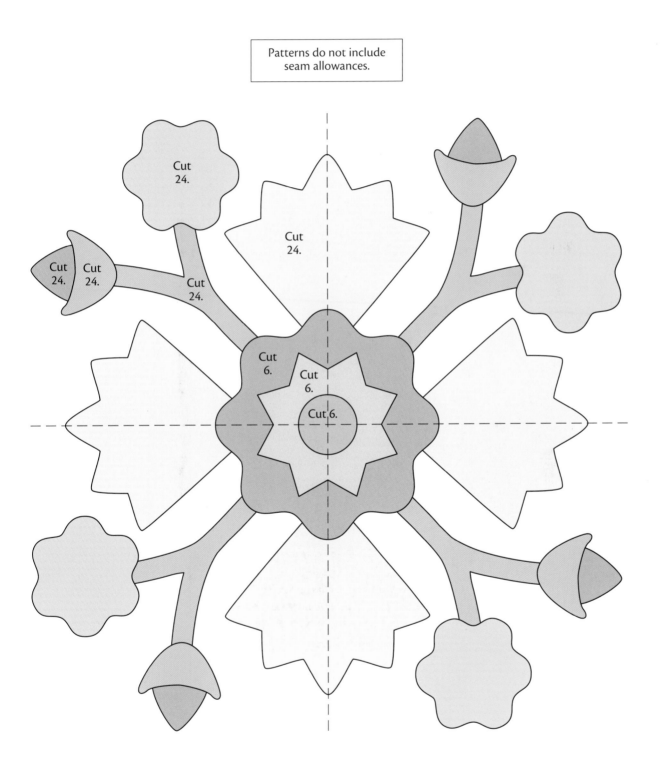

Oak Leaf Glory

Inspired by the colors of the border print, a stylized Oak Leaf block is reminiscent of our grandmother's quilts. Perfect your appliqué skills while making this lovely quilt.

Finished quilt: 16" x 20"

Materials

1 fat quarter of light fabric for background
1 fat quarter of floral for border
6 fat eighths of fabric in assorted colors for
    appliqués
1 fat quarter of fabric for binding
1 fat quarter of fabric for backing
18" x 22" piece of batting

Cutting

From the floral, cut:
1 strip, 2½" x 12½"
2 strips, 2½" x 20½"

From the binding fabric, cut:
4 strips, 1¾" x 20"

Appliquéing the Quilt

1. Use a marking pencil to draw a grid of six 6"
squares on the right side of the light fat quarter that
will be your background. Be sure that the markings
can be easily removed later. The background will
be trimmed to 12½" x 18½" after the appliqué is
complete. See top right.

2. Referring to "Needle-Turn Hand Appliqué"
on page 90, prepare the appliqué pieces for your
favorite method using the pattern on page 84.

3. Mark the placement of the appliqué pieces on
the background. Appliqué the pieces in place on
each square.

4. Press the appliquéd quilt center from the wrong
side and trim it to 12½" x 18½".

5. Add the floral 2½" x 12½" border strip to
the bottom of the quilt; press. Add the floral
2½" x 20½" border strips to the sides; press.

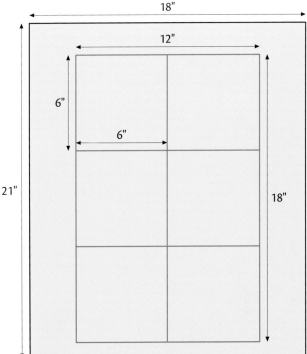

6. Layer the quilt top, batting, and backing. Baste
the layers together and quilt as desired. Add a line
of quilting along the grid lines that you drew to
make the "blocks" stand out. Add the binding and
enjoy.

Pattern does not include
seam allowance.

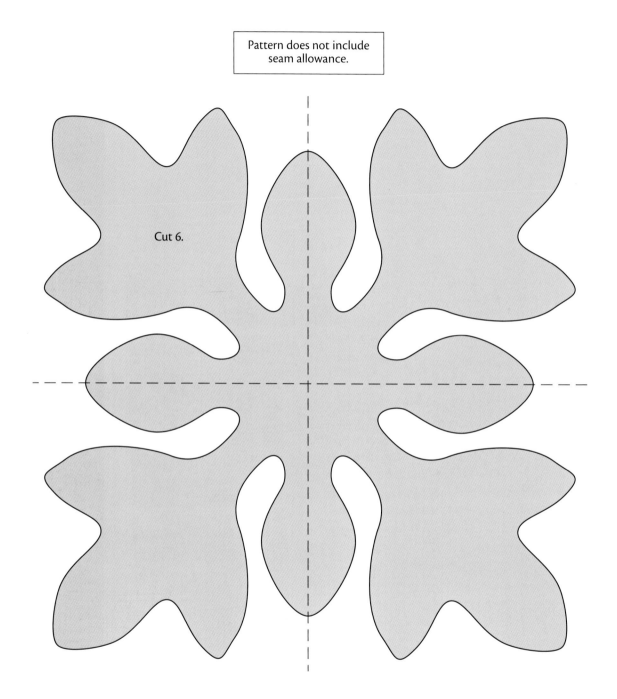

Cut 6.

Vase of *Flowers*

The stylized appliqué motifs and bold use of colors was popular during the mid-1800s. To further enhance the aged appearance of the quilt, the geometric quilting design crosses the entire surface of the quilt including the appliqué pieces.

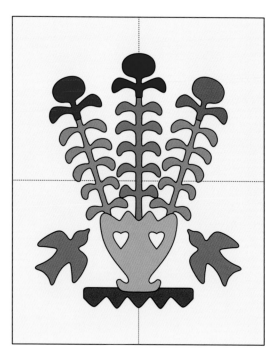

Finished quilt: 16" x 20"

Materials

1 fat quarter of light fabric for appliqué
  background
1 fat quarter of red print for sawtooth border
  and appliqués
1 fat quarter of gold plaid for vase and flat
  piping
Assorted scraps of red and green prints for
  appliqués
1 fat quarter of fabric for binding
1 fat quarter of fabric for backing
18" x 22" piece of batting

Cutting

From the light fabric, cut:
1 rectangle, 17" x 21"

From the red print, cut:
2 strips, 2" x 20½"
2 strips, 2" x 16½"

From the gold plaid, cut:
2 strips, ¾" x 20½"
2 strips, ¾" x 16½"

From the binding fabric, cut:
4 strips, 1¾" x 20"

Appliquéing the Quilt

1. Referring to "Needle-Turn Hand Appliqué" on page 90, cut and prepare the appliqué pieces using the patterns on pages 87 and 88.
2. Fold and lightly press the light background rectangle in fourths.
3. Align the dashed lines on the appliqué pattern with the creases in the background fabric. Mark the appliqué pattern on the background fabric.
4. Arrange the appliqué pieces on the background and appliqué them in place using your favorite method. Trim the quilt to 16½" x 20½".

5. Use the sawtooth border pattern on page 88 to mark the pattern across the red 2" strips. Part of the charm of this quilt is the casual nature of the appliquéd border. Accuracy and consistency in cutting are not important. Don't worry about the corners being the same either.
6. Cut the sawtooth border, adding a ³⁄₁₆" seam allowance for hand appliqué. Position the borders on the quilt and baste the straight edges in place.

Baste.

7. Appliqué the borders in place on the quilt.
8. Press the appliquéd quilt center from the wrong side, or use a pressing cloth.
9. Layer the quilt top, batting, and backing. Baste the layers together and quilt as desired. Add the binding and enjoy.

Note: To add the flat piping, fold the gold plaid strips in half, right sides together, and press. Insert the piping between the quilt and the binding and stitch it as you machine sew the binding.

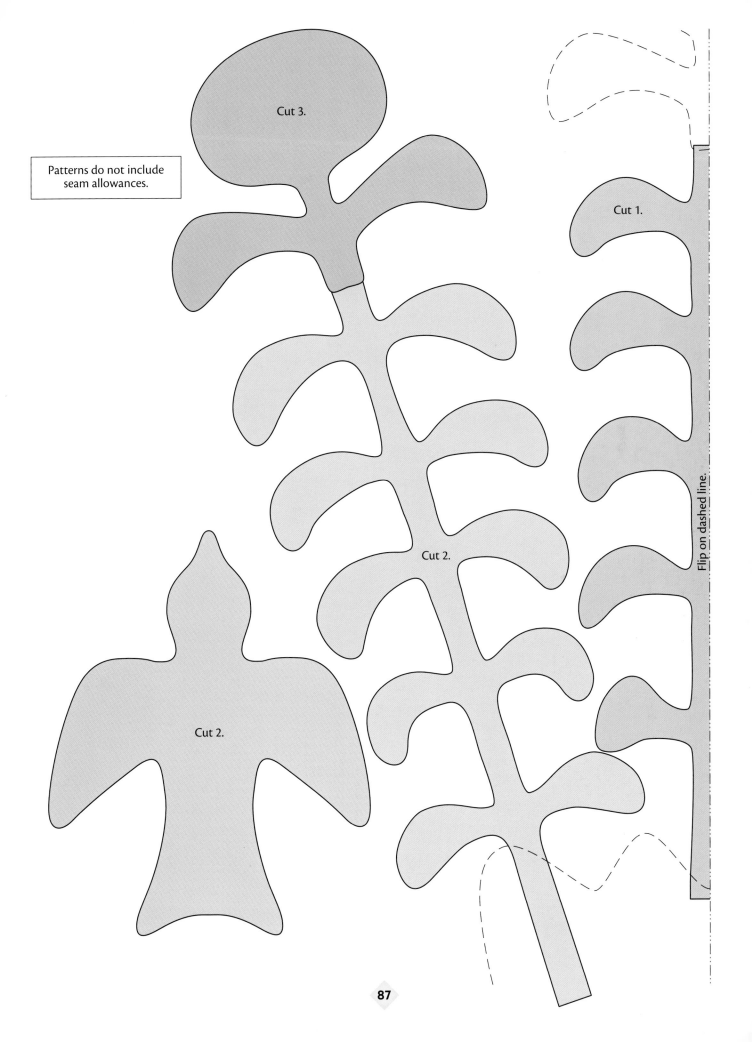

Cut 3.

Patterns do not include
seam allowances.

Cut 1.

Cut 2.

Cut 2.

Flip on dashed line.

87

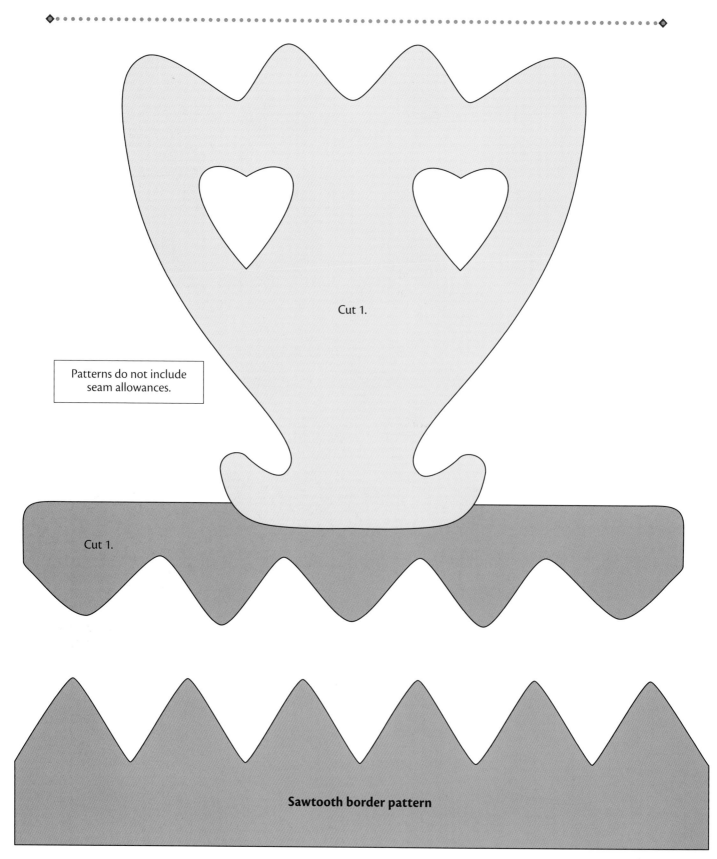

Cut 1.

Patterns do not include
seam allowances.

Cut 1.

Sawtooth border pattern

Quiltmaking Basics

In this section, I've included a brief overview of the quiltmaking process. This section assumes you are familiar with basic rotary cutting and piecing techniques. If you are not, I suggest that you take a class at a local quilt shop or refer to your favorite quilting reference book.

Fabric Selection

Color and fabric selection is always important when making a quilt. Typically, color is the first thing you notice when viewing a quilt, then the design of the quilt, and finally the craftsmanship. The fabrics used in small quilts can be as varied as their makers. All styles and colors of fabrics are appropriate for small quilts, from reproduction to traditional to contemporary fabrics. Start by selecting colors or fabrics that really appeal to you and build your palette of colors and fabrics from there.

Below are some guidelines to consider when selecting your fabrics. This is one of my favorite parts of the process. Remember to have fun!

• Start with one multicolored fabric that you love and select colors from its color scheme. Add a variety of fabrics to coordinate with it. Use the color dots along the selvage to help you isolate the colors from the print.

• Strive for a balance in the pattern, color, and value of your fabric selection.

• Include a variety of prints such as floral, geometric, pictorial, paisley, toile, solid, tone-on-tone, mottled, batik, polka dot, plaid, striped, checked, and reproduction prints. The shapes in the prints may have a sharp, dramatic image or a soft, blended image.

• To emphasize the pattern or shapes in a block or quilt, select fabrics that are not heavily patterned such as tone-on-tone, solid, hand-dyed, batik, variegated, mottled, subtle, small-scale prints, and prints that act as solids (printed fabric made from different values of one color). Heavily patterned fabrics demand their own emphasis.

• Check the lines within your fabric choices to be sure that they look good together. Lines within fabric can be directional, such as diagonals and zigzags, or they can be soft, flowing, curvy lines.

• Lines and shapes within fabrics can create restful areas or areas of dramatic movement. Repeating lines and shapes within a fabric creates rhythm and repetition.

• Check for the scale or size of the print in the fabric. Include a variety of small-, medium-, and large-scale prints. When working with small quilts, the scale of the fabric print is relative to the size of the quilt. What is considered a large-scale print for a small quilt isn't really that large when compared to large-scale prints used in larger wall hangings or bed-sized quilts.

• Include a variety of colors such as red, pink, rust, orange, peach, yellow, gold, green, teal, blue, maroon, purple, brown, white, cream, gray, or black.

When working with one color, such as green, consider extending your colors around the color wheel—use yellow greens and blue greens as well within a predominantly green quilt. To expand a blue palette, include blue green, blue, and blue violet; using peach, pink, red, and maroon will extend a red palette.

• Consider the intensity of the colors. Adding a few bright colors in small amounts will add highlights and spark to a quilt without overpowering everything else.

• Create a balance of values from lights to darks or work within a smaller value range such as pastels or dark fabrics. When working with a limited value range, use differences in colors rather than value to differentiate the individual pieces and blocks.

• To create depth within a quilt, add dark colors or values. However, adding pure black tends to sharpen and define the colors around it instead of achieving the depth you desire. Instead, use a less intense, neutral black or a black fabric that has other colors printed on it. Another option is to use dark fabrics in other colors such as a deep navy, green, maroon, purple, charcoal, or brown.

• For a limited color palette, such as blue and white, try using several blue and white fabrics instead of just two fabrics. Perhaps add an unexpected red or purple patch to add further interest.

• Consider the overall theme or style of the quilt you wish to create. Using a palette of pastel colors will create a soft, delicate appearance. Bright, pure colors exude a dramatic, bold appearance. Civil War–era reproduction fabrics and plaid fabrics will create an aged, country-style quilt. Bold, heavily printed fabrics enhance a folk-art quilt style.

• To create a charming, primitive appearance, randomly select fabrics. Don't overmatch your colors, fabrics, or patterns. Colors can be slightly uncoordinated and a bit scrappy. Consider cutting plaid and striped fabric slightly off grain.

• Use a variety of fabrics versus a few safe fabrics. Use some dramatic, nontraditional fabrics and colors along with your time-honored favorites. Using a few "ugly" fabrics brings character to small quilts.

• Finally, examine your fabric choices from a distance. Values and fabric designs read differently from a distance than they do close up. Remove fabrics that just don't seem to fit and any fabrics and colors that lack unity and harmony with the others. Preferring scrap quilts, I tend to have 25 or more fabrics available when cutting the pieces for a small quilt. Ultimately, not all fabrics I've selected will be used in the project. Even though I initially chose some fabrics, it doesn't mean I have to use them. I can change my mind, and so can you!

Needle-Turn Hand Appliqué

I prefer to appliqué by hand using the needle-turn method. For this, use a long, fine Sharp (appliqué) needle as a tool to turn under the raw edge of the appliqué piece as you stitch. Use your favorite method, if you prefer, adjusting the instructions as

necessary. For fusible appliqué, reverse the patterns when tracing.

1. Cut the background fabric ½" to 1" larger than the desired unfinished size to accommodate any fraying, distortion, and shrinkage that tends to occur during the appliqué process.

2. Fold and lightly press the background fabric in fourths to mark the center, folding and pressing one crease at a time.

3. Place the background fabric on top of the appliqué pattern. (Trace or photocopy the original pattern in the book to make this easier.) Line up the creases of the background fabric with the dotted line of the appliqué pattern and then trace the appliqué pattern on the front of the background fabric using a light marking pencil. A light box is helpful for tracing. If you don't have one, you can trace on a window.

4. Trace the appliqué pattern pieces onto template material. Carefully cut the appliqué templates following the traced lines.

5. Trace around the appliqué templates onto the right side of the chosen appliqué fabrics using a marking pencil or fabric marker. Cut out the appliqué pieces, adding a ³⁄₁₆" turn-under allowance for hand appliqué. Cut stems or vines on the bias, adding a ³⁄₁₆" turn-under allowance on each side of the finished stem (or a total of ³⁄₈" to the finished stem width).

6. Arrange the appliqué pieces on the background fabric to check for color placement and selection. Adjust the colors as needed. Remove the appliqué pieces from the background fabric; then pin the first appliqué piece to the background.

7. Select an appliqué needle in the size and length that works best for you. I use a size 10 Sharp needle for appliqué, but some quilters prefer straw needles. They're slightly longer than Sharps. Thread the needle with a thread color that matches the appliqué fabric. Tie a knot in one end.

8. Use the tip of the needle to turn under the raw edge of the appliqué piece, folding the turn-under allowance back so the tracing line disappears. Bring the needle up from the wrong side of the background, just inside the fold. Then insert it into the background just outside the fold. Come up into the fold again about ⅛" to ⅛" away. Continue to stitch the appliqué piece in place with a blind stitch. The stitches should be nearly invisible on the top and appear as a slightly slanted running stitch on the wrong side of the background fabric. The appliqué-stitch length should be small enough to securely hold the appliqué in place, especially when the quilt will be regularly washed. It is better to create slightly larger stitches that are enjoyable to do than to labor over creating smaller stitches. Practice will enable you to create smaller stitches.

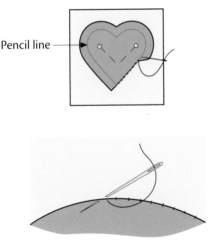

Pencil line

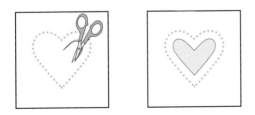

Appliqué stitch

9. Trim away background fabric behind the appliqué shapes, leaving a ¼" seam allowance. This is optional, but recommended, especially when the appliqués will be quilted through.

10. Press the appliqué pieces and background fabric from the wrong side and lightly press on the front side. Use care not to distort the fabric when pressing.

11. Trim and square up the background fabric to the required unfinished measurement.

Tips for Successful Hand Appliqué

• When stitching, pull the appliqué stitch tight enough so that the edge of the appliqué shape cannot be pulled away from the background, but not so tight that the fabric puckers.

• Clip inner curves and points when you get to them to avoid fraying. Cut deeper curves almost to the stitching line, while shallower curves can be clipped two or three fabric threads away from the stitching line.

• Fold the turn-under allowance on corners and points almost like you would fold wrapping paper on the ends. Trim the excess turn-under allowance on the tip of the points.

• Reinforce curves with 3 or 4 extra stitches and points with 1 or 2 extra stitches.

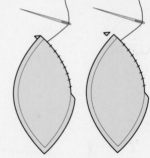

• Generally, stems and leaves are stitched first while flowers are stitched last. When one appliqué piece overlaps another, stitch the bottom piece first.

• When appliquéing the stems, finger-press the ³⁄₁₆" turn-under allowance along both edges of the bias stem. Stitch the inside curve of the stem in place first to the background fabric. Needle turn the other edge and stitch in place.

Cutting and Machine Piecing

All measurements in the cutting lists include a ¼" seam allowance, and the instructions are written for rotary cutting. Accuracy in cutting is very important since small blocks offer very little room for error. Also, due to the relatively small size of the pieces in the blocks, it is very important that your seam allowances are sewn accurately. Review the tips below for helpful hints.

• Use a size 10 or 11 Sharp needle in the sewing machine.

• Use a neutral-colored thread such as cream, tan, or gray that blends with the fabrics being sewn.

• When stitching many pairs of pieces together, chain piecing makes sewing go faster and usually results in greater accuracy. Sew the first pair of patches together, and then without cutting the thread, sew another pair and continue stitching until all pairs have been stitched. Cut the pairs apart, trimming dog-ears as needed.

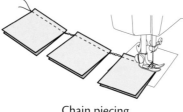

Chain piecing

• Proper pressing helps with sewing accuracy. Press the seam allowances toward the darker fabrics or in the direction that creates the least bulk. Remember to press each seam flat first; then press the seam allowances to the side (or open).

• Be careful to press lightly in an up-and-down motion to avoid distorting the pieces.

• I often press many of the final seams within a block open to more evenly distribute the fabric in the seam allowances and to produce sharper points. When pressing seam allowances open, reduce the stitch length on your sewing machine to strengthen the seams.

Simple Design Wall

It's very helpful to have a design wall when arranging your quilt blocks. It's also very easy to make one for the small quilts in this book. Mine is made of a 24" x 30" foam-core board covered with a piece of leftover cotton batting. I prop it against a wall when arranging the pieces for a quilt. The board is easily moved to my sewing table with the blocks in position when I'm ready to sew.

Layering, Basting, and Quilting

1. Press the quilt top and mark the desired quilting lines on the right side.

2. Cut a layer of batting and backing a few inches larger than the finished top. I prefer thin cotton batting to create a flat, aged appearance.

3. Lay the backing wrong side up on a flat surface. Add the batting and the quilt top, right side up, to create the quilt "sandwich." Baste with thread for hand quilting or safety pins for machine quilting to hold the layers together.

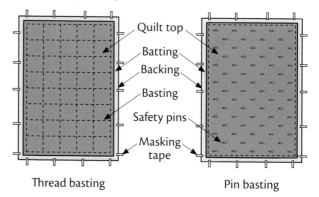

Quilt top
Batting
Backing
Basting
Safety pins
Masking tape

Thread basting   Pin basting

4. Quilt by hand or machine. If you hand quilt, take small, even running stitches, beginning in the center of the quilt and working out using a quilt hoop or frame to secure the quilt.

5. Remove basting thread or pins after quilting.

Binding

I cut binding strips 1¾" wide for all of the quilts in this book. This results in a finished binding width of about ¼". I like the look of a narrow binding on these small quilts. You'll need to cut enough strips to go all the way around the quilt plus 6" to 8" for joining the strips and mitering corners. Since the quilts all measure 16½" x 20½" before adding binding, the distance around the quilt will always be 74". Therefore, four strips cut across the 21" width of a fat quarter should be enough.

Frame It!

Try framing one of the quilt tops in a ready-made 16" x 20" frame. Use it for a gift or for easy, fast, and fun decorating!

1. Stitch the ends of the binding strips together on the diagonal. Trim the seam allowances to ¼" and press them open.

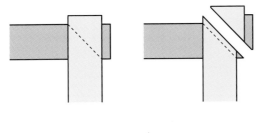

2. Fold and press the binding strip in half length-wise with the wrong sides together. Fold in one end of the strip on the diagonal.

Fold line

3. With the raw edges of the binding and quilt top even, stitch the binding with a ¼" seam allowance, leaving a 6" tail unsewn. Stop sewing ¼" from the corner of the quilt. Backstitch and clip threads.

4. To miter the corner, fold the binding strip straight up on the diagonal. Finger-press the diagonal fold, then fold the unsewn binding over itself, lining up the raw edges. Begin stitching from the edge of the quilt.

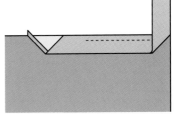

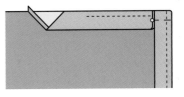

5. Continue sewing around the quilt, mitering each corner in the same manner. Overlap the end of binding with the starting point by 1". Hand stitch the ends together using a blind stitch.

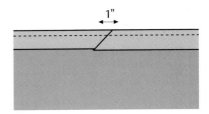

6. Cut away the excess binding. Trim the excess batting and backing even with the unfinished edge of the quilt top.

7. Fold the binding to the back of quilt, covering the machine stitching; hand sew it in place using a blind stitch.

Signing Your Quilt

Quilts are works of art and should be treated as such. Like any artist, sign your quilt or make a label and sew it on the back. Include your name, city and state, date of completion, and any other information that ensures the continued legacy of the quilt and artist who created it.

About the *Author*

With a bold leap of faith, Lori Smith started her quilting business, From my heart to your hands, in 2003 to share her passion for the art of quiltmaking. A native of Minnesota, she is a self-taught quilter of 25 years, artist, designer, and author who holds degrees in the fine arts and education. Her design philosophy explores and builds upon the quilt legacy of our ancestors. Lori enjoys combining hand appliqué with machine piecing for a stunning combination when creating her traditionally inspired quilt designs. She has designed more than 225 small quilts, in addition to her larger quilts. With endless design inspirations, she continues to create even more quilts, utilizing her extensive collection of fabrics. Her passion for quilting includes all aspects—the design process, fabric and color selection, hand appliqué, machine piecing, hand quilting, and especially sharing her love of quilting with others through her patterns. Lori also enjoys photography, nature, interior design, and collecting antiques. To see additional quilts created by Lori, visit her website at www.frommyhearttoyourhands.com.

New and Best-Selling Titles from

 That Patchwork Place®

America's Best-Loved
Quilt Books®

 *Martingale*®
& COMPANY

America's Best-Loved Craft & Hobby Books®
America's Best-Loved Knitting Books®

APPLIQUÉ
Applique Quilt Revival
Beautiful Blooms
Cutting-Garden Quilts
Dream Landscapes
Easy Appliqué Blocks—NEW!
Simple Comforts—NEW!
Sunbonnet Sue and Scottie Too

BABIES AND CHILDREN
Baby's First Quilts
Baby Wraps
Let's Pretend
Snuggle-and-Learn Quilts for Kids
Sweet and Simple Baby Quilts

BEGINNER
Color for the Terrified Quilter
Happy Endings, Revised Edition
Machine Appliqué for the Terrified Quilter
Your First Quilt Book (or it should be!)

GENERAL QUILTMAKING
Adventures in Circles
American Jane's Quilts for All Seasons
Bits and Pieces
Bold and Beautiful—NEW!
Cool Girls Quilt
Country-Fresh Quilts
Creating Your Perfect Quilting Space
Fig Tree Quilts: Fresh Vintage Sewing—NEW!
Folk-Art Favorites—NEW!
Follow-the-Line Quilting Designs
    Volume Three
Gathered from the Garden
The New Handmade
Points of View
Prairie Children and Their Quilts
Quilt Revival
A Quilter's Diary, Written in Stitches
Quilter's Happy Hour
Quilting for Joy
Remembering Adelia—NEW!

Simple Seasons
Skinny Quilts and Table Runners
That Patchwork Place® Quilt Collection—NEW!
Twice Quilted
Young at Heart Quilts

HOLIDAY AND SEASONAL
Christmas Quilts from Hopscotch
Comfort and Joy
Holiday Wrappings

HOOKED RUGS, NEEDLE FELTING, AND PUNCHNEEDLE
Miniature Punchneedle Embroidery
Needle-Felting Magic
Needle Felting with Cotton and Wool

PAPER PIECING
Easy Reversible Vests, Revised Edition
Paper-Pieced Mini Quilts
Show Me How to Paper Piece
Showstopping Quilts to Foundation Piece
A Year of Paper Piecing

PIECING
501 Rotary-Cut Quilt Blocks
Favorite Traditional Quilts Made Easy
Loose Change
Maple Leaf Quilts
Mosaic Picture Quilts
New Cuts for New Quilts
Nine by Nine
On-Point Quilts
Quiltastic Curves
Ribbon Star Quilts
Rolling Along

QUICK QUILTS
40 Fabulous Quick-Cut Quilts
Instant Bargello
Quilts on the Double
Sew Fun, Sew Colorful Quilts
Supersize 'Em!—NEW!

SCRAP QUILTS
Nickel Quilts
Save the Scraps
Scrap-Basket Surprises—NEW!
Simple Strategies for Scrap Quilts
Spotlight on Scraps

CRAFTS
A to Z of Sewing—NEW!
Art from the Heart
The Beader's Handbook
Card Design
Crochet for Beaders
Dolly Mama Beads
Embellished Memories
Friendship Bracelets All Grown Up
Making Beautiful Jewelry
Paper It!
Trading Card Treasures

KNITTING & CROCHET
365 Crochet Stitches a Year
365 Knitting Stitches a Year
A to Z of Knitting
All about Knitting
Amigurumi World
Beyond Wool
Cable Confidence
Casual, Elegant Knits
Crocheted Pursenalities
Gigi Knits…and Purls
Kitty Knits
Knitted Finger Puppets
The Knitter's Book of Finishing
    Techniques
Knitting Circles around Socks
Knitting with Gigi
More Sensational Knitted Socks
Pursenalities
Simple Stitches—NEW!
Toe-Up Techniques for Hand-Knit
    Socks, Revised Edition
Together or Separate